"With this remarkable handbook, [...] near impossible: a thorough guide [...] inspirational as it is practical. Wh[...] this book is richer, still, in wisdom[...]

—M. WAYNE BROWN, MDiv, LMFT, psychotherapist; author of *Water from Stone*

"Comprehensive, street-wise, biblical, accessible, truth-filled, and compassion-centered. Every caregiver, from group leader to senior pastor, should keep this handbook close by at all times."

—BILL DONAHUE, PhD, pastor of leadership development, Willow Creek Community Church, South Barrington, Illinois

"Every believer who seeks to minister to cancer patients, grieving parents, husbands and wives in crisis, and victims of abuse will find this superb handbook a true guide for Jesus-like wisdom and compassion. Barb Roberts offers the distilled wisdom of decades of firsthand pastoral care experience. This practical work of spiritual direction will prove to be an invaluable tool in obeying Christ's call to bear one another's burdens."

—DOUG WEBSTER, PhD, professor of pastoral theology, Beeson Divinity School, Birmingham, Alabama

"This book is a rich resource for those who desire to embody the healing presence of God to family and friends suffering through the losses and sadness of life. Barb Roberts has lived the experiences of a caregiver dependent on God for so long that she cannot help but overflow with sound and practical wisdom born of years of first listening to God and then listening to those in pain. The book is like a useful toolbox, pulled off the shelf on numerous occasions to prepare yourself for a work of caring service. In the modern world of mobility and the evaporation of natural support networks, this equipping of the church and its people to be a caring community could not be more crucial."

—ROBERT CUTILLO, MD, Inner City Health Center, Denver, Colorado

"Barb Roberts is uniquely gifted to encourage people who are hurting. Drawing upon her wealth of personal experience, she has blessed us with this practical, compassionate, and Christ-centered guide."

— BRAD MEULI, president/CEO, Denver Rescue Mission

"What can pastors and caretakers do when one of the members of their congregation has a personal crisis? Grab this handbook as a reference! When you are called on to support a hurting person, you need an easy-to-use reference to remind you of the specifics of serving those in that particular situation. This is the book that will be used over and over by people who want to be wise in caring about others."

— RUTH GONZALEZ, PhD, psychologist and assistant professor, Lewis and Clark College, Portland, Oregon

"For ten years, I have watched Barb Roberts help those who hurt. When it comes to entering a crisis, she is very wise. She has raised the standard of care at our church and will help you do the same."

— DONALD SWEETING, PhD, senior pastor, Cherry Creek Presbyterian Church, Englewood, Colorado

"*Helping Those Who Hurt* is an excellent resource for those who want to help loved ones and friends in crisis but lack knowledge with how to help in a meaningful way. Roberts's rich insights reflect years of experience in ministering to those who are hurting. Her descriptions of the thoughts and feelings of those in difficulty are especially valuable, as they help you 'put yourself' in that suffering friend's place."

— DR. JEFFREY JEREMIAH, stated clerk, Evangelical Presbyterian Church, Livonia, Michigan

HELPING THOSE

Who Hurt

A HANDBOOK FOR CARING AND CRISIS

BARBARA M. ROBERTS

NAVPRESS

NAVPRESS●

NavPress is the publishing ministry of The Navigators, an international Christian organization and leader in personal spiritual development. NavPress is committed to helping people grow spiritually and enjoy lives of meaning and hope through personal and group resources that are biblically rooted, culturally relevant, and highly practical.

For a free catalog go to www.NavPress.com
or call 1.800.366.7788 in the United States or 1.800.839.4769 in Canada.

ISBN: 978-1-60006-382-4

Cover design by studiogearbox
Cover photo by iStock

Some of the anecdotal illustrations in this book are true to life and are included with the permission of the persons involved. All other illustrations are composites of real situations, and any resemblance to people living or dead is coincidental.

Unless otherwise identified, all Scripture quotations in this publication are taken from the *Holy Bible, New International Version*® (NIV®). Copyright © 1973, 1978, 1984 by International Bible Society. Used by permission of Zondervan. All rights reserved. Other versions used include: *The Living Bible* (TLB), copyright © 1971, used by permission of Tyndale House Publishers, Inc., Wheaton, IL 60189, all rights reserved.

Library of Congress Cataloging-in-Publication Data

Roberts, Barbara M., 1942-
  Helping those who hurt : a handbook and resource guide for caring and crisis / Barbara M. Roberts.
     p. cm.
  ISBN 978-1-60006-382-4
  1. Peer counseling in the church. 2. Suffering--Religious aspects--Christianity. 3. Pastoral counseling. 4. Church work. I. Title.
  BV4409.R63 2009
  253'.7--dc22

                                    2008036630

Printed in the United States of America

3 4 5 6 7 8 / 19 18 17 16 15 14

My heart overflows with thanks to . . .

*Liz Heaney—my editor, for her wise counsel,
making this a more helpful tool.*

*Cherry Creek Presbyterian staff—my pastors Don Sweeting,
Marty Martin, and Bruce Finfrock, for their commitment to
Caring Ministry, and to Callae Dykstra and LaRue Fleming, for
partnering with me in reaching out to the hurting.*

*My family—my husband, Ken, without whom I would not have
been able to be in pastoral care ministry for all these years. My
children, Kirk and Jay, Gene and Gwen, and Kim and Joe, who
love me and believe in me. My grandchildren—Kelle and Jordy;
Jake, Mitchell, and Jeremiah; Tyler, Cooper, Coby, and Peyton,
who bring me great joy. For all of them, my heart's desire is to
leave a legacy of godly care for those in need.*

Contents

Part 4: DEATH

Part 5: GRIEF

Part 6: TROUBLED MARRIAGES AND DIVORCE

AUTHOR'S NOTE

Whether you are in ministry or simply want to help a family member, friend, colleague, or neighbor, you can use this guide as an easy reference for how to care for and support those who are walking through difficult circumstances.

As a caregiver, it's critical that you never betray the confidence of the person for whom you are caring unless you have reason to believe that person is in danger of harming others or himself. It's been said that "a secret is something that is shared with just one person at a time." Christians often share confidences under the guise of "sharing a prayer request," as if it "sanctifies" their betrayal. It doesn't.

The call to care for others sometimes carries with it the unrealistic expectation that you will know everything you need to know to minister to the wounded. This book will give you some basic tools and information that you can utilize and refine. Each section focuses on some of the common problems and issues that people face, and includes the following:

- General information about the issue or problem.
- Specific information about what to do or say for the person in need of care.
- Specific advice the caregiver can offer to the person in need.
- Information written directly to those in crisis, to be passed along as needed. (These pages can be photocopied.)
- An annotated list of resources I've found helpful as a pastoral caregiver; they provide more detailed information than I am able to offer here.

The demands of caregiving can be draining, so as caregivers we need someone to confide in who will help us carry the burden. Jesus is, of course, our Chief Burden-Bearer, but Galatians 6:2 also reminds us that we must have others to help bear our burdens. For me, that person is my husband, Ken. He listens, encourages, supports, and prays for me. Find someone who will do the same for you.

Always remember to prayerfully place those you are caring for into the hands of the One who really *does* know the perfect cure for the specific pain.

A Note About Depression

Hurting people often struggle with depression, as it is a natural reaction to stress and tension. It can affect anyone, at any time. Depression ranges from mild to severe.

- *Mild* depression, which is often called "the blues," is usually brief and does not seriously interfere with normal activities.
- *Moderate* depression brings feelings of hopelessness that are more intense and longer-lasting than mild depression.
- *Severe* depression is identified by a loss of interest in the outside world and serious, prolonged behavioral changes.

Your role as a caregiver is to listen to, support, and pray for those struggling with depression. Individuals with either moderate or severe depression should get the help of a professional counselor. Be quick to recognize when you are "in over your head," and make a referral, providing resources and even offering to accompany the person to the first counseling visit.

Keep in mind that professional support is something that should be recommended *in addition* to your help, not *instead of* your help. Whether by phone, e-mail, or personal visits, be consistent in your contact with anyone you refer to a professional. Depressed people need hope, and it's very important that you remind them that God is a God of hope (see Romans 15:13). Listen to the psalmist crying out to God in his depression:

Out of the depths I cry to you, O Lord;
    O Lord, hear my voice.
Let your ears be attentive
    to my cry for mercy.
If you, O Lord, kept a record of sins,
    O Lord, who could stand?
But with you there is forgiveness;

therefore you are feared.
I wait for the LORD, my soul waits,
and in his word I put my hope. (Psalm 130:1-5)

PART 1

Illness and Hospital Visitation

He gives strength to the weary
and increases the power of the weak.
Isaiah 40:29

MINISTERING THROUGH ILLNESS AND A HOSPITAL VISIT

Because of the brevity of today's hospitalizations, pastoral caregivers have a narrow window of time in which to make an in-patient visit. Hospitalization is a crisis, both to the patient and to the family—a crisis that extends far beyond the person with the medical problems. To cope with the situation, everyone involved will need to draw on resources he or she doesn't ordinarily use. The patient and family may need your help in defining and implementing the use of these resources.

Many of those you minister to in this setting will be experiencing this trauma for the first time. They may be blindsided by things that are not directly related to their physical problem—for example, assault to their modesty and dignity, depression over the losses they are experiencing, loneliness, fears, and even anger.

People who are hospitalized may have lots of visitors, but no one to talk to about their concerns and feelings. The presence of one who cares and understands some of what they are experiencing, *and who really listens*, can be very comforting and encouraging.

One of the most important things you can do is help patients deal with their feelings about the illness, such as anger ("Why did God allow this to happen to me?") or fear ("What will happen to my kids if I am not around for them?"). This may require you to deal with strong feelings and to be open to a patient telling you his or her story. You may also need to be comfortable sitting in silence with someone who needs to have you there but may not want conversation.

God calls us to minister to the sick; let us do so with His guidance and His sensitivity.

Differences Between a Social and a Pastoral Visit

While a patient may have many visitors, there are few who actually *minister* through the visit. If you are in ministry, it is vital for you to bridge the gap between a social and a pastoral visit.

Social conversation concentrates on the following:

1. Discussing external subjects: weather, work events, local events.
2. Maintaining a congenial atmosphere.
3. Maintaining personal comfort through avoiding uncomfortable topics.
4. Sharing stories and mutual experiences.
5. Being pleasant and positive.
6. Generalizing and universalizing (for example, talking about what "they" say or what "people" do).
7. Discussing religion, but centering only on differences between churches, services, or clergy.

Pastoral conversation concentrates on the following:

1. Understanding the patient's needs.
2. Accepting tension areas. (The seriousness of the surgery or illness has little to do with how seriously the patient views the situation.)
3. Offering comfort through empathizing with the patient's pain.
4. Helping the patient talk about himself or herself.
5. Being understanding and empathic.
6. Asking specific questions: What do you think? How are you feeling about that? Where is God for you in this?
7. Asking if you can share a word of Scripture and pray for the person.
8. Identifying the patient's spiritual or religious needs by paying attention to what is said, to what feelings are expressed,

to how questions are answered, and to the patient's body language. For instance, clenched teeth, tears, frequent sighs, and white-knuckled fists are signs of fear or anger. If you see any of these signs, say, "Are you afraid?" or "Tell me about the tears."

Some Possible Spiritual/Religious Needs

Need for community (church and friends). Many patients are isolated, with very little support system around them, so ask them specifically about their support system and offer to assist in connecting them to others. After a patient is discharged from the hospital, follow up with your offer of assistance. Depending on the need, you might ask someone in a small group in your church to invite the person to the group. Eventually the patient could be drawn into the community of the larger church body.

Need to tell one's story. When you are visiting patients as a pastoral caregiver, ask open-ended questions, such as "Who have you been able to talk to about all of this?" "Where is God for you right now?"

Need for reconciliation (with church, family, God, others). As you listen to a patient's story, pay attention to unresolved relationships and the need for forgiveness or to forgive others.

Need to express brokenness, hurt, and pain to God. To open up to you, people need to feel that you are comfortable with expressed pain, whether it is expressed in anger or tears. Ask patients if they would like to have you talk to God about their hurt and pain. Then, pray, either with a step-by-step prayer, asking them to repeat phrases, or pray and quietly wait for them to join in when ready.

Need for meaning and purpose in life (hope). During the time that the patient is grappling with questions—Why did I get cancer? What will happen to me when I can't work because of my illness and subsequent treatment? Where is God in all this?—listen to the person's questions and remind her that God has a purpose and plan for her life (see Jeremiah 29:11) and that He is faithful (see 1 Corinthians 10:13).

Need for expression of grief, anger, fear, especially as it relates to God, church, or values. Be available to listen to expressions of anger or fear. In fact, if you sense that a patient is struggling with one or more of these emotions, ask, "Are you afraid?" "Are you kind of ticked at God right now?" If the patient answers you honestly, listen respectfully, without judgment. If the patient is not ready or willing to express emotions, redirect the conversation toward safer ground.

Need for awareness of God. Ask the patients for whom you are caring, "Where is God in all of this for you right now?" Then listen to just where they are. This is not the time for deep theological explanations; this is the time for simple spiritual truths. Tell patients, "God loves you. He really loves you."

Need for connectedness with God, communion with God (prayer, friends, answers). Ask patients if you can pray for them right there, right then. Then pray, but first ask what they would like you to pray about specifically. As you listen to their prayer needs, you may hear things that you might not think to pray about.

Need for grace and acceptance. Ask God to help you not to judge or be critical of those for whom you are caring. Accept them right where they are—with their fear, anger, frustration, or whatever the immediate struggles are.

Need to feel adequate, competent, autonomous. Though you cannot help others feel adequate or competent, you do have the opportunity to protect their dignity by respecting their privacy and encouraging them to make whatever decisions are in their power to make.

Need to feel that someone is in control. Remind patients that God made them and understands them (see Psalm 139). Show them passages such as Hebrews 12:2-3, which talks about Jesus being the author and perfecter of our faith, and Hebrews 4:15, which emphasizes that Jesus understands our pain and struggles.

Need for confession and for inner healing from emotional hurt and feelings of fear or of being punished, abandoned, or alienated. Some patients may struggle with the need for forgiveness, and you as the pastoral caregiver have the opportunity to be sensitive to their need to confess their sins to God and to remind them that God has promised to forgive (see 1 John 1:9).

Need for comfort or to be freed from some form of bondage. Second Corinthians 1:3-6 reminds us that we go through struggles and suffering to be able to comfort others, so tap into your own experiences in being comforted as you offer comfort as a caregiver.

Need for inspiration, positive motivation, enthusiasm. As a pastoral caregiver, be an encourager and supporter, sharing favorite Scriptures, readings, or poems that are meaningful to you and may be to those who are ill. Music can also be an inspiration to those who are struggling.

Dos and Don'ts for the Hospital Visitor

Hospital visits can be spiritual in nature. If you are visiting someone in the hospital . . .

Do

1. Dress in appropriate attire.
2. Check at the nurses station *first*.
3. Make a visit *before* surgery, if at all possible.
4. Be cheerful, but not jovial. Allow the patient to express feelings.
5. Allow the patient to choose topics of conversation, and listen carefully.
6. Be encouraging and optimistic, but don't give false hope.
7. Ask permission to read a suitable passage of Scripture and to pray. This shows respect for the patient and his or her needs. Ask the patient for specifics to include in your prayer.
8. Be sensitive to questions, apprehensions, or struggles the patient may be experiencing, especially terminally or seriously ill patients.
9. Be sensitive to the patient's desire to be touched or not touched. If you have any doubt, ask, for instance, "May I put my hand on your shoulder while we pray?"
10. Respect confidentiality of all information. Don't force information on a patient who is emotionally, physically, or spiritually ill equipped to handle it. Be cautious about asking too many questions to satisfy *your own* curiosity.
11. Be prepared to step out of the room if a physician or nurse comes in to examine, give an injection, or otherwise treat the patient, or if the patient needs to use bathroom facilities.
12. Stay with a relative who is alone at the hospital until the surgery is over and the surgeon gives a report to that family member.

13. Visit seriously ill or terminally ill patients at least once a week, either in the hospital or at home, and more often as death becomes imminent.

Don't

1. Don't try to diagnose the illness or offer medical advice.
2. Don't help the patient out of bed without hospital personnel.
3. Don't undermine the patient's confidence in his or her physician or the treatment being received.
4. Don't give your evaluation of the patient's condition.
5. Don't relate similar cases in your experience or discuss personal problems.
6. Don't open closed hospital doors; you may be embarrassed, and so will the patient.
7. Don't sit on the bed with the patient, visit at mealtime, or stay too long.
8. Don't express repugnance when experiencing odors, the sight of blood, or other unpleasantness.
9. Don't probe into areas of privacy or say you know exactly how the patient feels.
10. Don't discuss church business, church politics, or church problems.
11. Don't give false hope to terminally ill patients.
12. Don't make decisions for the patient or family members that they should make themselves.
13. Don't preach or lecture, and do not be afraid of silences.
14. Don't encourage patients or families to do what they do not want to do or do not believe would help.
15. Don't analyze where the patient is in the dying process, and don't attempt to move or push a patient or family to the "stage" you think is next or preferred.

Potential Problems of Patients

Issues and potential problems often become magnified during illness and hospitalization. When you are caring for someone who is in the hospital or rehabilitation facility, be aware of the potential for the patient to experience some of the following problems.

Physical or Emotional Problems—or Both

- Loss of personal freedom
- Being subject to orders of medical personnel
- The presenting symptoms of the illness
- Crippling injuries, scars, wounds, infection
- Grief and loss issues related to illness
- Ignorance of human anatomy
- Ignorance of rules of health and hygiene
- Congenital defects
- Fear of the unknown, of pain, of depersonalization, of lack of control
- Fear of the process of the hospitalization, such as the fear of anesthesia, the fear of tests, or the fear of surgery
- Conflict with authority figures
- Boredom
- Difficult living conditions, such as roommate issues
- Depersonalization (loss of identity as a person)
- Strange procedures

Financial Problems

- Cost of hospitalization or cost of co-pays
- Loss of employment
- Loss of income

Social and Interpersonal Maladjustment Problems

- Conflicts in family, community, and peer relationships
- An asocial personality or antisocial personality
- Belligerence or anger

Job and Vocational Problems
- Unemployment
- Being unemployable
- Misemployment
- Youth and inexperience
- Approaching retirement, or being in retirement

Sexual Problems
- Premarital or marital problems
- Homesickness and loneliness
- Tension, inhibition, repression, exhibitionism, lack of control

Religious or Spiritual Problems
- Doubt, a lack of faith, weakness of faith; agnosticism; atheism
- Feelings of guilt; religious legalism
- Feeling a need to be punished for sin
- Inability to pray or worship
- Relationship to church or organized religion
- Fear of the future; fear of dying; fear of the afterlife

Philosophical Problems
- A lack of acceptance of own humanity
- The unfairness of creation
- The question of why there is sickness, suffering, evil, and death
- The question of whether the patient's life has purpose, or whether attempts at purpose are futile
- The validity of euthanasia or suicide

Recommendations
1. You need wisdom, discernment, and sensitivity in observing, listening to, and responding to any of the above problems the patient may be struggling with.

2. Some problems may be obvious and surface quickly in caring conversation between caregiver and patient. Do not be judgmental but be grace-filled in responding to any of these problems.
3. If you observe needs that the patient does not express, refer to "Differences Between a Social and a Pastoral Visit" for help (pages 17–20).

Much of the above information is adapted and used with permission from Rev. Doug Overall, chaplain and pastor at an evangelical Presbyterian church in St. Louis, Missouri.

SPECIAL PROBLEMS OF TERMINAL ILLNESS FOR PATIENT AND FAMILY

The patient and family may have to deal with:

- ❧ Numerous remissions and relapses and the psychological reactions that arise with each.
- ❧ Lengthened periods of anticipatory grief (the continual ups and downs — the emotional roller-coaster ride for patient and family).
- ❧ Increased financial, spiritual, social, physical, and emotional pressures.
- ❧ The progressive decline of one's loved one and the emotional responses of family members to this decline.
- ❧ A longer period of uncertainty.
- ❧ Dilemmas about treatment choices.
- ❧ Intensive treatment regimens and their side effects.
- ❧ Post-treatment anxiety. (What next?)
- ❧ Loneliness, for both the patient facing this final journey and for the family anticipating separation.
- ❧ The need to be able to talk when desired and to be assured that someone will listen to the patient's "story."
- ❧ The difficult decisions surrounding when to call in hospice care.
- ❧ End-of-life issues, such as family discussions about discontinuance of life support. *Special note*: If a family has never openly discussed these issues, their trauma will be multiplied and amplified.

Recommendations

1. Be open to the patient's terminology. Remember, you cannot push, pull, or rush a person from one stage in the grieving process to another. For instance, if a person is in denial, it is

not your role to force him or her to accept the fact that the illness is terminal.

2. Be available to spend extra time with the dying person if he or she wants you there. If you don't know if you are wanted, ask! "Would you like to have me stop by this afternoon for a visit and to pray with you?"

3. Be sensitive to the patient's desire to be touched or not touched.

4. Ask what specific things the patient would like to have you pray about; then *pray* with and for him or her.

5. Ask about specific concerns of family members. There may be some assistance you can offer. This information will also give you direction from the patient about the things he or she would like to have you address in prayer.

6. Ask about and read favorite Scripture passages. If the patient can't think of any, Psalms 139, 91, and 23 are good choices.

How to Care for Cancer Patients

If you are visiting someone who has cancer:

1. Treat the patient as much as possible as you did before the diagnosis, including continuing to laugh together.
2. Show empathy, not pity.
3. Talk directly about cancer. Asking about it demonstrates you're not afraid of it. It gives the patient the opportunity to talk about it.
4. Include the patient in conversations about your own life as a way of encouraging him or her to feel connected to the world. *Don't monopolize the conversation.* Be careful not to trivialize the patient's need to discuss his or her own situation.
5. Provide as much practical help as you can—get creative! For example, if a female patient has experienced hair loss from chemotherapy, offer to go with her to pick out a wig or to purchase hats or scarves.
6. Celebrate milestones, such as holidays and completions of treatment.
7. Don't be afraid that you're going to "catch it." Cancer is not contagious. Be sure to continue physical contact—touching or hugging.
8. Tell success stories about cancer, but only when appropriate.
9. Don't concentrate on your own or another's disaster story.
10. Hang on to hope for the patient.
11. Remember there are millions of ex-cancer patients.

Caring for Someone with HIV or AIDS

Here is some general information about HIV and AIDS:

- ❦ Human immunodeficiency virus (HIV) leads to AIDS (acquired immunodeficiency syndrome).
- ❦ HIV disables the immune system in many complex ways.
- ❦ HIV reproduces itself, infecting other cells throughout the body.
- ❦ The infected T4 cells die or are unable to function properly.
- ❦ HIV attacks the immune system, which is gradually weakened.
- ❦ HIV causes the body to lose its ability to fight off infections and illnesses.
- ❦ Factors such as stress, poor nutrition, and other lifestyle issues may further weaken the immune system.
- ❦ An AIDS diagnosis results from a combination of HIV infection and opportunistic infections or cancers.
- ❦ HIV is a fragile virus and cannot live for long outside the body. As a result, the virus is not transmitted through day-to-day activities, such as shaking hands, hugging, or contact with a toilet seat, drinking fountain, doorknob, and so on.

In addition, here are some concerns that are unique in the care for persons with AIDS. (Many of these same issues are experienced to a lesser degree with people who learn that they are HIV positive.)

Feelings of Profound Loss of Control and Helplessness Due To . . .
- ❦ The disease process and the person's own physical well-being.
- ❦ The overwhelming number and depth of emotional issues and decisions.
- ❦ The loss of personal privacy and lifestyle.
- ❦ The incongruence of knowledge and experience. (In earlier stages AIDS patients may appear healthy.)

❧ Little or no experience of death. According to the National Prevention Information Network, half of all new HIV infections are believed to occur in people under the age of twenty-five.

❧ Multiple losses of friends to AIDS.

Recommendations

1. Don't see the patient as a victim. See the patient as a person with AIDS (PWA).
2. Reinforce the PWA's sense of control whenever possible or appropriate.
3. Hope is needed; nevertheless, avoid false hope.
4. Early mortality rates have changed with recent medical advances and changes in treatment. Point out those advances and changes in treatment.
5. Support the need for confidentiality.
6. Sit with the PWA who is anxious. Help the PWA name and face his or her anxieties. Be willing to walk alongside the PWA in the tensions that come with this disease.
7. Reframe questions. Help the PWA ask, "What does give me hope?" "What do I hope to give others through my life and through my death?"

Homophobia (the Fear and/or Hatred of Homosexuals)

❧ If a PWA struggles with homosexuality, he or she may be homophobic.

❧ Every person in our culture has some homophobia.

❧ Many homecare services refuse PWAs, due to homophobia.

Recommendations

1. Examine your own attitudes and prejudices. View PWAs first and foremost as God views them — as people He loves and died for.
2. Be attentive to and challenge oppressive comments and behavior.

Societal Attitudes Toward Addiction and Prostitution

- ❦ Many segments of our society assume that a PWA must be either an addict or a prostitute.
- ❦ Addicts and prostitutes are often seen as marginal, the throwaway portion of society. As a result, the PWA may have internalized feelings of worthlessness.

Recommendations
1. Recognize the value God places on the person.
2. Examine your own attitudes and prejudices.
3. Do not be judgmental.

Special Needs Of . . .

Children with AIDS
- ❦ Often from low-income situations that offer few resources
- ❦ Often unwanted; called "throwaway" children
- ❦ May need to be placed in foster homes

Women with AIDS
- ❦ Often from low-income situations that offer few resources
- ❦ Often indirectly infected; often risk unsafe sexual activity
- ❦ AIDS in women not as fully researched because of a lower number of infected women

Men with AIDS
- ❦ Often infected because of having sex with multiple partners or prostitutes
- ❦ May be especially lonely because they may have no lasting relationships

Recommendations
1. Recognize the potential in you for judging. At the same time, remember that "there is now no condemnation for those who

are in Christ Jesus" (Romans 8:1).
2. Show compassion and friendship.
3. Pray with and for the PWA.

Feelings of Shame and Guilt

❧ The PWA may have feelings of exposure around having a previously private or hidden lifestyle divulged.
❧ The PWA may have issues of guilt about his or her past.

Recommendations

1. Encourage the PWA to express his or her feelings.
2. Listen and empathize.
3. Help PWAs to distinguish rational from irrational guilt.
4. Be Jesus to them.
5. Be reliable and consistent.
6. Give yourself permission to experience discomfort.
7. Recognize that the PWA has the same fears, struggles, and pain as those with other kinds of terminal illnesses.

Special Concerns of Those Who Contract AIDS from Something Other Than Sexual Contact

❧ Often called innocent victims
❧ Often need to work through guilt and trust issues because of being deceived by someone close to them
❧ May be receiving support from people who condemn someone the PWA loves

Recommendations

1. Consider what *innocent* means; this virus is no respecter of persons.
2. Show compassion — unconditional caring — for the PWA.

PART 2

Crisis

*And my God will meet all your needs according to
His glorious riches in Christ Jesus.*

PHILIPPIANS 4:19

Life Crises and Coping

Crises are inevitable. In fact, life could be described as a series of crises. We all experience crises of varying types and degrees of intensity throughout our lifetime.

Webster defines a *crisis* as a "turning point." A crisis, then, comes about because of a change, usually one perceived as hazardous. Before a crisis begins, a person is in a relative state of equilibrium. Picture a triangle, sitting on its base, a flat surface. When the crisis hits, our life triangle tips up on end, no longer on level ground. As caregivers to those in crisis, we have the privilege of being used by God to help restore a sense of equilibrium.

Life-changing events, which set the stage for crises, may come because of the natural maturing process, or they may come as a surprise. While circumstances may have been building for a time, the precipitating event marks the actual beginning of the crisis state.

Crises that develop because of unexpected happenings are called accidental crises. These result from events that bring too much change over too brief a period. If this change is perceived as a threat (and it frequently is), then a crisis is likely to develop. Examples of events that may precipitate an accidental crisis include:

- Serious illness
- An automobile accident
- Loss of a limb
- Getting fired from one's job
- Death of a child

The intensity of the crisis will depend on several factors, including:

- The suddenness of the onset
- The health of the person at the time, both physical and emotional
- Other difficulties in the person's life

- The kind of support available and the effectiveness of that support
- Previous crises and learned coping mechanisms
- The severity of the crisis
- The person's relationship with God and unresolved past issues
- The amount of advanced warning

Common emotional responses to a crisis include crying, anger, guilt, and remorse. Common physical reactions include stomach pains, tightness in the throat, numbness and tingling in the extremities, headaches, and a stiff neck. Behavioral disorders, such as difficulties in sleeping, eating, and working are also common. Obviously, the crisis state, which yields disorganization and confusion, can affect many aspects of a person's life at one time.

For the most part, people experience the crisis state with all its intensity for a limited time, usually four to six weeks. That six-week period is a window of opportunity that opens the widest in the first twenty-four hours of the crisis. Whoever jumps in first has the greatest opportunity to affect the direction of the change that will result.

As a caregiver, it is important that you recognize your own capabilities and limitations in crisis care and that you have other people available to share the load. This involves a team — usually acquaintances of the individual in crisis — who can come around the person in crisis, carrying various parts of the load.

Scripture offers us insight into how to help those in crisis. According to Galatians 6:1-5, when there is a burden too big for another to handle alone, we are to help carry that burden. Later on in that same passage we are told that each should carry his or her own load. Others must share the burden; the load involves those areas of personal responsibility that the individual must work through with God.

Another crucial guideline for crisis work is not to accept a third party's definition of a situation. Check out the facts! This is especially significant in referral situations, when a third party defines the crisis of someone else. *All crises have the characteristic of urgency, but not all crises are emergencies*. People often take an urgent situation and convert it into an emergency, resulting in irrational response. An urgent matter requires immediate *attention*. An emergency requires immediate *action* to prevent dire consequences. A crisis may involve an emergency, or it may not. Check out all pertinent information when asked to become involved in a crisis.

As an intervener in a crisis, you may not have to do much to provide the needed help. Simply being there to listen and to assist in exploring the options may be what is needed to help a person turn a crisis into an opportunity for growth. Without intervention, the hurting person is likely to opt for the course of least resistance, which all too often results in inadequate adjustment to the event.

Don't forget to pray and to ask for God's help. I can't emphasize enough how imperative it is to pray with and for people through the course of the crisis. That is where the real power is. The apostle Paul declared that we are weak but He is strong: "My grace is sufficient for you, for my power is made perfect in weakness" (2 Corinthians 12:9).

Our confidence comes in understanding that God's purposes and ways are much higher than ours, regardless of life's difficulties. There is purpose in our suffering:

> In this you greatly rejoice, though now for a little while you may have had to suffer grief in all kinds of trials. These have come so that your faith — of greater worth than gold, which perishes even though refined by fire — may be proved genuine and may result in praise, glory and honor when Jesus Christ is revealed. Though you have not seen him, you love him; and even though you do not see him now, you believe in him and are filled with an inexpressible and glorious joy, for you are receiving the goal of your faith, the salvation of your souls. (1 Peter 1:6-9)

It is a rare privilege, indeed, to be allowed to intervene in another's crisis.

THE UNIQUENESS OF EACH CRISIS

Each of the following scenarios is a precipitating event that could lead to a crisis:

- A young mom locks her keys in the car with the engine running. She needs to pick her kids up from school in fifteen minutes.
- A grandmother is babysitting four of her grandchildren when it becomes apparent that the very large family dog is dying, and Mommy and Daddy are out of town.
- A dad of five young children loses his job.
- A young man is rushed to the hospital just in time for an emergency appendectomy.
- A mom and dad are dealing with a very rebellious teen.
- A young couple has found out yet again that she is not pregnant, and they so desperately want a baby.
- A mom and dad get a police call about their teenager in the middle of the night.
- The doctor gives a spouse an unexpected medical diagnosis.
- A man named Job in the Old Testament loses his children, servants, animals, health, and house.

HELPFUL INFORMATION FOR THOSE IN A CRISIS

Share the following information with those in crisis, and help them to recognize God's available presence, love, and power.

1. Pray! Pray by yourself and allow others to pray with you.
2. Ask God for truth telling. Recognize what is real and true about this situation and what is false. Remember that we have an enemy who is, as Scripture says, "the accuser of [the] brothers" (Revelation 12:10). Satan will try to distort and contort whenever and wherever possible.
3. Face your "demons." Recognize that this is a crisis.
4. As soon as possible, find someone you trust to help.
5. Allow yourself to "be" where you are, with whatever emotions you are experiencing.
6. Be aware that multiple issues often accompany any life crisis.
7. Allow yourself and your caregiver to separate the issues you are facing.
8. Prioritize, recognizing what must be dealt with first.
9. Take personal responsibility for your part in this situation.
10. Recognize what is changeable and what is unchangeable.
11. Use the small-step approach. Taking small steps is the first part of the solution in resolving the situation.
12. Do not isolate from family and friends even though this is the tendency in a crisis.
13. Do not allow yourself to go down the "what if" road too far. It is a dead-end street!
14. Take care of yourself: rest, hydrate, nourish.

STEPS TO FOLLOW DURING A PUBLIC CRISIS

To be prepared for a public crisis, develop an emergency plan for your church or organization that includes the following:

1. Identify emergency personnel: the decision-making team, the central communication team, and the spokespeople.
2. Identify safety procedures.
3. List emergency agencies that must be contacted.

When the crisis occurs:

1. Define the type and extent of the crisis immediately.
2. Document all the facts of the precipitating event. Write down the location, date, and time of the incident, the type of happening, the cause, and all the persons involved.
3. Notify all those with a need to know about what is happening and designate a central source of communication to coordinate information.
4. Identify a spokesperson to handle press inquiries in those cases where the news media is involved.
5. Release information promptly, but only when the facts have been verified.
6. Notify members of your organization as soon as reasonable once all information is gathered and verified. For instance, in a school, a whole-school announcement may be sent to teachers to read to their individual classes. In a church, there should be an announcement at the next worship service or all-church meeting. There should also be communication through church-wide e-mails and telephone trees.
7. Ensure the safety of all present.
8. Notify appropriate family members.

Information from Ruth Gonzalez, PhD, psychologist, Lewis and Clark College, Portland, Oregon (February 2008).

COMMON RESPONSES OF PEOPLE IN CRISIS

It is difficult to predict what anyone, including yourself, might do in a crisis. Some people collapse immediately, while others discover inner reserves that enable them to cope with even prolonged periods of intense crises. In either case, there is a need for caregiving.

Emotionally a Person May Respond to a Perceived Crisis With . . .

- Self-preoccupation
- Anxiety (this can lead to poor judgment)
- Helplessness
- Dependence on others
- Loss of self-esteem
- Anger (over the whole situation — sometimes at God)
- Tears
- Guilt and remorse
- A reexamination of his or her relationship with God
- A temporary loss of faith

Physically a Person May Respond to a Perceived Crisis With . . .

- Stomach pains
- Tightness in the throat
- Numbness and tingling in the extremities
- Headaches
- Stiff neck

Behaviorally a Person May Respond to a Perceived Crisis With . . .

- Disorganization and confusion
- Difficulty sleeping, eating, and working
- Decreased efficiency

Recommendations
Obviously, the crisis state can affect many aspects of a person's life at one time. Caregivers need to make contact with those in crisis and show concern through the ministry of presence. The immediate goal is to get the person in crisis through the initial "crisis window," helping him or her find appropriate resources.

DOS AND DON'TS IN CARING FOR SOMEONE IN CRISIS

When you are caring for someone in crisis . . .

Do

1. Pray as you are driving to meet the person. Ask God for wisdom. The apostle Paul wrote, "I can do everything through him who gives me strength" (Philippians 4:13). Remember, your strength and wisdom come from Him, not yourself.

2. Demonstrate calmness, concern, and acceptance. (This does not mean that you do not have your own emotions to deal with during the crisis.)

3. Find out about the situation—when the crisis started and what went on before it began.

4. Listen long, hard, and without interrupting. People in crisis need to tell their story and tell their story and tell their story—multiple times, in various ways.

5. Let your demeanor be appropriate. Scripture tells us to "rejoice with those who rejoice; mourn with those who mourn" (Romans 12:15).

6. Allow emotions to surface. If you are uncomfortable with tears, remember that is your issue to work through.

7. When several people are involved in a crisis, deal with the most anxious person first, helping reduce his or her anxiety.

- Help the person explore the present situation by describing feelings, thoughts, and plans.

- Help the person narrow down what the real problems are, with an inventory of his or her resources and a list of alternative resources. For each alternative, help the person decide what is feasible, what will really help, and what is easiest to accomplish.

- Remember: People in crisis are very often suggestible. Don't push your own solutions, and be cautious even about making strong suggestions.

8. Ask the person to identify those individuals who could comprise a "share the care" team—a group of friends and family who are available to help with a variety of details and tasks. The team needs one person to be the coordinator (this could be you), who organizes meals, phone calls, and so on.

9. Ask for permission to pray with the person in crisis. Allow God to guide you.

10. As appropriate, share Scripture without bombarding the person. Again, allow God to guide you in this.

11. Research and then connect the person to appropriate resources.

12. Give the person permission to grieve and struggle.

13. Take the person and the crisis seriously. Never minimize what a person is going through.

14. Remember that the severity of the crisis depends on many things, including other issues in the person's life, his or her perception of the severity of this crisis, and the support network surrounding him or her.

15. Help the person be safe, which may include moving her to a place where she is not isolated.

16. Keep the details of the situation confidential.

17. Be available. When asked for help, respond as quickly as possible. Keep in mind that the first caregiver on the scene in a crisis is often the one most appropriate to do follow-up care.

Don't

1. Don't judge, condemn, or blame.

2. Don't use clichés! For example, don't say, "Isn't it a blessing that he is no longer suffering?" or "Look on the bright side!"

3. Don't encourage a person to think about something else. (He or she needs to be able to think about and process the crisis.)

4. Don't assume responsibility for the person or his crisis; you are responsible to, not responsible for. (It is not up to you to "fix"

the person; rather, it is up to you to be available to support and encourage.)

5. Don't think it is your job to eliminate another's pain.

Types of Abuse

To abuse means to:

- ✤ Use wrongly or improperly; misuse
- ✤ Hurt or injure by maltreatment
- ✤ Assail with contemptuous, coarse, or insulting words

Abusive behavior happens in many forms, combinations, and patterns, including these six general categories:

- ✤ *Emotional abuse* (humiliation): One person uses fear to steadily grind down another's self-worth and self-respect.
- ✤ *Spiritual abuse*: The mistreatment of a person who is in need of help, support, or empowerment with the result of weakening, undermining, or decreasing that person's spiritual empowerment.
- ✤ *Physical abuse*: One person causes physical pain and suffering, cripples, endangers, hurts, injures, kills, maims, or traumatizes another. (One form of physical abuse is domestic violence, which is covered in part 8 of this guidebook.)
- ✤ *Psychological abuse*: One person uses the following tactics to corrode the foundations of logic on which another makes decisions and takes action, such as:

  - Playing mind games to steadily convince another that he or she is crazy
  - Using "brainwashing" techniques to manipulate another's will
  - Creating a constant state of anxiety to increase tension

- ✤ *Sexual abuse*: One person forces another to have *any* unwanted sexual contact.
- ✤ *Social abuse*: One person deprives another of social contact to increase his or her dependence and compliance and to decrease resistance.

HOW TO RECOGNIZE AND RESPOND TO A CHILD'S DISCLOSURE OF ABUSE

Children disclose abuse in a variety of ways. Sometimes they disclose it through direct and specific communication, but unfortunately that is not usually the case. More often children will disclose through indirect means, for example, saying things like "Our neighbor wears funny underwear" or "My brother bothers me at night," or asking you to promise to keep a secret. After an episode of physical abuse, a child might say something like "Mommy says I'm really clumsy. I fall down the stairs a lot." Or "I didn't mean to be bad last night."

If you suspect that abuse has taken place, but the child does not disclose it at all, follow your "gut." Listen to this inner concern and ask the Spirit of God for wisdom in revealing the abuse and relating to the child.

It is important to listen, encourage, and assure the child. Compassionately ask specific questions if the child's comments seem to be covering up an underlying problem. For instance, say, "Honey, tell me what happened just before you fell down the stairs." Or "You know, it's okay to tell someone else a secret if a big person is hurting you." Be careful that your questions do not relay any accusation you may feel toward the abuser; the child may believe he or she caused the abuse.

Let the child know you want to help him or her. If the child asks you "not to tell," gently respond by saying, "I will only tell so that, together, you and I can get you help." Be careful that your queries don't lead to certain responses—for instance, naming a specific individual you suspect may be the guilty party. Never finish a child's sentences or fill in the blanks.

If you suspect abuse, it is your responsibility to report it to the Department of Social Services or the local police department. It is *not* your job to confront the suspected abuser. Social service agencies have the training and expertise, as well as the best interests of the child in mind. You need to be available to continue to give care to the child as well as to the family: listening to, praying for, and spending time with them.

Here are some dos and don'ts if a child tells you that he or she has been sexually abused:

Do

1. Believe the child.
2. Find a quiet, private place to talk to the child. If the issue is physical abuse, discretely look for bruises.
3. Take a positive approach to the problem. Reassure the child that he or she has done the right thing by telling someone.
4. Listen to the child. Let him or her talk openly about the situation.
5. Rephrase important thoughts for clarification, using the child's vocabulary.
6. Allow the child to go at his or her own pace. It may be easier for the child to disclose by using a doll or puppet, or by drawing or writing about the incident.
7. Ask only for information that will clarify your suspicion. Proper authorities will gather the detailed information.
8. Tell the child that there is help available, and then get the help both you and the child need.
9. Reassure the child that you will do your best to protect and support him or her.
10. Let the child know you must report the abuse to someone who has helped other children like him or her and their families.
11. Report the incident to the proper authorities. Contact your local police or Department of Social Services.
12. Let the child know what will happen when the report is made (if you have appropriate information).
13. Seek out your own support person (or persons) to help you work through your feelings about the disclosure (if needed).

Don't

1. Don't promise confidentiality.
2. Don't express panic or shock.
3. Don't convey anger or impatience if the child is not ready to discuss the abuse.
4. Don't make negative comments about the perpetrator or get into a moral lecture about the incident.
5. Don't disclose the information indiscriminately. Tell only those adults who need the information to protect and support the child.

PART 3

Aging

They will still bear fruit in old age,
they will stay fresh and green,
proclaiming, "The LORD is upright; he is my Rock,
and there is no wickedness in him."

PSALM 92:14-15

THOUGHTS ON AGING

According to the Federal Interagency Forum on Aging Related Statistics, by the year 2030 the percentage of persons in the United States age sixty-five or older is projected to climb to 21 percent of the total population. The average life expectancy in the United States has gradually increased over the years, from forty-seven years in 1900 to seventy-four years today. If a person reaches age sixty-five, life expectancy climbs to eighty-one years. According to the U.S. Census Bureau, since 2000, more than 100,000 people have lived to be one hundred years of age. In the years to come, there likely will be an increase in the average age as well as an increase in the over-sixty-five population as a group. It has been said that the current sixty-five is the previous fifty-five.

Our society marginalizes the elderly and frequently goes so far as to support many inaccurate stereotypes and myths about them. One of the greatest myths is that old people are senile. It is true that severe deterioration of the brain occurs in some older people, but those who are truly senile are only a small percentage of the total number of older persons whom others label as senile. Much of what we call senility may actually be depression, grief, lack of social stimulation, drug tranquilization, or lack of a proper diet.

Some people inaccurately apply the saying "You can't teach an old dog new tricks" to older persons. I have worked with seniors in the past few years who have created and implemented new areas of ministry.

If you are a caregiver to an elderly person, you have the opportunity to:

- Recognize the wisdom and potential of older persons.
- Encourage and support their endeavors; for example, an elderly friend of ours began a home-based Web business. We encouraged him and offered suggestions when he asked for help.
- Treat him or her with respect.

- Learn from his or her experience — for example, ask questions about his or her business experience, parenting, marriage experience, faith journey.
- Learn by hearing his or her stories.

It's been said that "aging is not for sissies." I agree. Typically, older persons are dealing with multiple losses, including the deaths of family members and friends. Saying good-bye to a close friend or relative involves losing a part of one's past as well as one's present. The death of contemporaries reinforces the inevitability of one's own mortality. Other stressors include economic inflation on a fixed income, health issues, increasing costs of health care, feelings of loneliness, and concerns and fears about future living situations. When helping folks who are struggling with many of these issues of aging, take their hurts, fears, and pains seriously.

When working with the elderly, keep in mind that "you're only as old as you feel." Or, as one chaplain at a nursing home put it, "It's not how old you are; it's how you are old." A sad truth is that if you tell people often enough that they are too old or not capable of certain accomplishments, they will probably begin to believe it.

Also remember that all people talk and think about the past. If older people talk more about the past than younger people, it may simply be because they have more past to talk about. This past may include people and events that are very enjoyable to talk about. It does not necessarily mean those people are living in the past. They may be leading active lives in the present. On the other hand, some older persons might be forced to live in the past if their present and future are taken from them. If meaningful activities are not available, the older person might gradually dwell more and more in the past, as there is less and less to do in the present.

A major crisis within this population is the crisis of retirement. This happens when the older person feels robbed of personal goals, financial self-sufficiency, or a real or perceived productivity. Retirement can bring unwanted idleness, which frequently stirs up anger within retired individuals. In addition, those who were healthy prior to their retirement sometimes suddenly begin to suffer digestive disorders, headaches, nervousness, irritability, and depression.

It is difficult for those who are younger to understand the grief that comes from the multiple losses suffered by their elders. The journey of grief experienced by older persons is very real and frequently produces depression. Yet often there is no one who is willing to walk beside retired people and to listen to their story. As a pastoral caregiver, you may be that person.

WHEN YOU CARE FOR ME, I'D LIKE YOU TO REMEMBER THAT . . .

Walk in the shoes of older people, and remember the following as you care for them:

- ❦ My steps are slower, and my mind and body may be frail.
- ❦ I may not hear as well as I used to. If I ask you to repeat something you said, I will appreciate your patience.
- ❦ My eyesight may be failing. I may enjoy having you read to me.
- ❦ My shaky hands may cause me to spill my coffee. I appreciate your help, but please protect my dignity.
- ❦ I appreciate visits, calls, cards . . . knowing that you haven't forgotten me.
- ❦ Sometimes I repeat myself; thanks for not calling it to my attention.
- ❦ I love to tell you about my past, if you'll just listen.
- ❦ I have things to offer you. I appreciate your remembering that and showing me respect. "Then they [the older women] can train the younger women to love their husbands and children, to be self-controlled and pure, to be busy at home, to be kind, and to be subject to their husbands, so that no one will malign the word of God" (Titus 2:4-5).
- ❦ I appreciate when you realize that I have burdens, and you ask me what they are and offer to pray with me and for me.
- ❦ It would be my great joy if my husband and children "would arise and call [me] blessed" (Proverbs 31:28).

HELPFUL INFORMATION FOR THE ELDERLY AND THEIR FAMILIES WHO ARE PLANNING FOR THE FUTURE

Sara and her husband recently attended a class for the Sandwich Generation, those people caught between their young children and their aging parents. She came because her mother was slowly becoming more confused and her father had begun to complain that he couldn't leave his wife alone for more than a few minutes. Sara was trying to juggle the demands of a busy young family with the needs of her parents.

Jerry, an only child, was faced with a difficult decision. His father, who lived in another state, was becoming very frail. Jerry thought he should bring his father to his community to live in a nearby nursing home; however, his father was adamantly resisting the idea of leaving his home of forty years.

Such situations are becoming more frequent as the population lives longer. Many elderly people are struggling to live in their house or apartment, either alone or with another frail, dependent mate. Sometimes they refuse help or even hide their need for help. Their fear of where their children might move them drives their judgment about revealing their needs.

The Saras and Jerrys of our country want their parents to remain as independent as possible for as long as possible. Many have little experience with social and health service providers beyond their physician, the hospital, and a nursing home (and few have ever visited a nursing home). When their aging parent is apprehensive of all three, the situation becomes very difficult.

What can family caregivers do? They can (and must) advocate for their aging parent. They can come up with a plan for what to do when the parent is in need of some assistance—perhaps a graduated plan of care. Whenever possible, include the parent in the plan to give that person a forum to express fears, wishes, and desires. Being included often eliminates the "dread factor," the fears brought on by questions like "What is going to happen to me?" "Where will I go?" "What if I run

out of funds?" "Will my family still care for me and come to visit me?"
Families need to discuss four primary areas:

- *Health matters*—the parent's health history, chronic diseases, or signs of illness.
- *Social concerns*—where will the parent live, the parent's feelings about physical and mental changes. Keep in mind that many complexes for seniors today provide a wide range of graduated care, from independent-living apartments to assisted care to skilled nursing care. Many also have hospice care available, should that be needed.
- *Legal issues*—legal tools, such as durable power of attorney, power of attorney for medical services, living wills, and trusts.
- *Financial planning*—whose signatures to include on bank accounts, property ownership, investments, income and assets; insurance alternatives, including medical and supplemental plans and long-term care policies.

Families must talk with their older relatives about such subjects. Such discussions can build trust and bring about deeper and more fulfilling relationships. This was the case for Sara and Jerry.

Sara and her parents finally sat down with a professional counselor to discuss how they could work together to relieve her father of some of the burden of caring for his wife. They concluded that a good plan would be to rent the apartment next door to Sara and her husband. This worked well because her mother felt comfortable because they were near when Sara's father left the apartment to go shopping or to the senior center. This simple solution included the parents in the decision-making process.

Similarly, Jerry learned about a variety of companion services available for his father. As his father became less able to manage his affairs, Jerry gradually assumed those responsibilities. When Jerry, his father, and a health service agency determined that living at home without supervision was no longer safe, they agreed that admission to a high-quality nursing home was appropriate. His father did not protest because he was part of the decision-making process.

Research clearly shows that when older people have the support of family or friends, they tend to remain living independently longer — that is, outside a nursing home.

The acronym CAN includes three important words for the elderly and their families: *choice*, *alternatives*, and *network*.

- *Choice.* For the elderly, choice may mean staying in their house longer than others deem it wise. If staying home is no longer possible, it may mean choosing which personal belongings to bring to the new living arrangement. Choices, large or small, give all of us a sense of control over our lives and a feeling of well-being. Being able to make personal choices allows the older person to maintain a sense of dignity and self-respect.
- *Alternatives.* The role of adult children or younger family members is to help identify the resources available to the older person. The frail elderly often are not able to plan or search for resources needed to improve their situation. This is the job of family and friends, who can recommend alternatives.
- *Network.* Those caring for a loved one should not try to do everything alone. It is important to work with a network. Sometimes this may be a spouse or a neighbor of the parent, but a caregiver should try to build a web of helpers, even if they are far away. A telephone call or a visit from a distant friend, son, daughter, or grandchild can make a difference and give a needed respite.

We honor God by responding with love, grace, and care to the elderly living in our midst. We do well to take instruction from the writer of Proverbs 3:1-3: "My son, do not forget my teaching, but keep my commands in your heart, for they will prolong your life many years and bring you prosperity. Let love and faithfulness never leave you; bind them around your neck, write them on the tablet of your heart."

Helpful Information for Those Caring for the Elderly

Giving care is a means of demonstrating Christlike love and concern. It is a spiritual gift that can have special meaning for the caregiver and the person being cared for.

Yet it can be taxing, both physically and mentally. At times you will feel at the end of your rope. However, God will give the caregiver strength to care as He intends. In his letter to the Corinthians, Paul declared that Jesus says, "My grace is sufficient for you, for my power is made perfect in weakness" (2 Corinthians 12:9).

For many, giving care to another person they feel close to fills their bucket with joy. This was the case for my neighbor. For well over two years, he spent from morning until well into the evening at the assisted-living facility where he had moved his dear wife. Prior to that, for as long as possible, he had cared for her in their home. He bathed her, fed her, helped her take whatever steps she could take, did the laundry, cooked, cleaned, and shopped. During this time, though we would talk at times about how hard it was to watch her struggle and suffer, he never complained about caring for her. He did whatever it took to serve her. His care for her was a beautiful picture of the servant love of Jesus, when He took on the garment of a servant and washed His disciples' feet.

However, if you are acting out of guilt, frustration, anger, or feelings of servitude, you will continue to struggle with resentment and anger toward the person for whom you are caring.

If you have a less-than-desirable relationship with a parent for whom you are caring, ask God for wisdom in resolving past conflicts as well as caring for your parent's physical needs. This is the time to decide to respond as an adult, rather than as a child who wants to be cared for. Your parent, sensing the difference, may begin to respond to you more as an adult to another adult. As a result, the two of you may help each other grow, and this new relationship may open opportunities for caregiving not previously possible.

Keep in mind that you may need counseling to help work through difficult, oftentimes hidden issues. A counselor can help you gain insights into your feelings as well as your parent's feelings. A counselor can also give the support and encouragement needed to try new ways of relating and to continue trying, even when early attempts fail.

Such experiences allow you to return the gift of caring you received many years ago.

How to Arrange a Homebound Person's Environment

There are many simple, inexpensive ways to make a home safer and more comfortable for a homebound person. Most of the equipment that may be needed to make these home adjustments can be bought at a hardware store; other adjustments can be made at no cost.

1. If the person is confined to bed, make sure a TV, radio, and telephone are accessible, as well as books and magazines, a reading lamp, call bell, water pitcher and glass, clock, and calendar.
2. Put the homebound person in a first-floor room, even if it means converting another room into a bedroom. If steps can't be avoided, try to install a ramp.
3. If possible, the room should be colorful and have a nice view.
4. The bathroom should be on the same floor, close to the person's room.
5. Install handrails in hallways and in bathrooms next to the toilet and in the shower. Bars make walking and getting up and down easier and safer.
6. Remove all elevated doorsills or install a ramp over them.
7. Eliminate shag carpets and slick floors and scatter rugs because of the danger of falls. Use only rugs with nonskid backs.
8. Make sure lighting is bright and adequate in the person's room and hallways.
9. In case of fire, prepare a plan of escape.
10. If the person is hard of hearing, turn the phone buzzer on loud or even install an amplifier on the phone.
11. Apply adhesive strips to the bathtub to prevent slipping.
12. Place a bench in the bathtub for easy and safe access.
13. Make wrist straps for those with walkers and canes to prevent dropping them. Straps can be made of tape, cloth, or rope.

14. Enlarge handles of knives, forks, and spoons to enable weak or arthritic patients to hold the utensils with less effort and more control. Try foam rubber, Velcro, cloth, or garden hose.

15. Plastic mattress covers protect a bed if a person eats or bathes in bed or is incontinent. Add a mattress pad over the plastic for comfort and to avoid slipping. Since these pads must be changed immediately when soiled, several will be needed.

16. Change door handles to a lever type rather than a knob to assist a weak or arthritic person.

17. Make sure their chairs have arms with which to push themselves up.

At more expense, the following equipment can be obtained to make a homebound person more comfortable. This equipment can be purchased or rented through a hospital, surgical supply store, or pharmacy. Depending on a person's medical condition, Medicare may reimburse for some of these items.

1. Buy or rent an electric or manual hospital bed to help the person sit up and get in and out of bed.

2. Purchase side rails for a regular bed if a person needs help getting in and out of bed or something to hold when turning over in bed.

3. To reduce the chance of bedsores, purchase a waterbed, air mattress, or foam padding for a person confined to bed.

4. Install a trapeze above a bed so the person can grab it to move around in bed.

5. Purchase an overbed table like those used in hospitals to facilitate eating, reading, and writing in bed.

6. Purchase an easy-lift chair, which is a mechanical or electric chair with a seat that lifts to make getting in and out easier. Secondhand chairs may be available from the Red Cross or Salvation Army.

7. Purchase a walker to increase safety and ease in walking alone.

PART 4

Death

Precious in the sight of the LORD
is the death of his saints.
PSALM 116:15

DEATH AND DYING

Death is a certainty for all of us. Our ability to help someone who is dying and the family of the dying person depends largely on our own attitudes regarding death. Some people avoid the subject as much as possible, feeling uncomfortable and even fearful in any discussion on the matter. Issues of our own mortality frequently surface as we care for the dying.

For this reason, it's wise as caregivers of the dying to examine our own theology of suffering. For example, try to recall one of your experiences with death. What elements of that experience were the most painful, and how has that experience influenced the attitudes you now have in regard to your own death or the death of someone close to you? What were some helpful and unhelpful things said to you during this process of the death experience?

It is important to understand that suffering is part of the Christian life. The "faith chapter," Hebrews 11, lists many who suffered for their faith and were commended for their faith through their suffering. Our main example for understanding our own theology of suffering is Jesus, "who for the joy set before him endured the cross, scorning its shame, and sat down at the right hand of the throne of God" (Hebrews 12:2).

To help someone going through the dying process, you must be able to comfortably discuss death and grief. Helpful theological components involve the recognition that God is sovereign, that God is loving, that suffering is part of life, that there will always be "why" questions, that we have a choice to grow through our suffering or to become bitter. We have the Comforter, and we learn in John 14 and 16 that He is with us always.

Keep in mind that the dying are people — people who are unique and who have distinct struggles. For instance, one person may want you to be a "silent presence" — someone to hold her hand, to pray with, and to just be there. Someone else may need more verbal communication, such as words of comfort and advice. It is important for you to understand these differences and to be tuned in to each particular person so that you can correctly discern his or her needs and desires.

Here are some gifts you can offer the dying patient:

1. To combat the feeling of isolation, offer the gift of your presence.
2. In recognizing the patient's feelings of frustration, anger, and sorrow, offer the gift of your listening ear.
3. To combat the anxiety surrounding "What will happen to my family?" help investigate available resources.
4. By recognizing the concern the patient may have regarding personal dignity, offer the gift of friendship.
5. To combat the many fears and feelings of hopelessness, offer the gift of eternal hope through Scripture and pray to the God of hope and comfort (see Romans 15:13).

Dr. Elisabeth Kübler-Ross, who died in 2004, has been recognized as one of the foremost authorities in the field of death and dying; she received her medical degree from the University of Zurich and was a prolific author on the subject of death and dying. She has identified *five stages of grief* that the dying experience.

1. Denial and disbelief
2. Rage and anger
3. Bargaining
4. Depression
5. Acceptance

These same reactions are present in the grieving process for the family of the dying. It is important to recognize that you, the caregiver, may be struggling with some of these stages yourself.

Though these stages are listed in a certain order, the dying person does not necessarily experience all of them, or experience them in order. For example, a person might react by bargaining with God for time

("God, if you will let me live until my grandchild is born . . ."), then become depressed, and later go back to bargaining yet again. Woven into all of that, a person may spend some time denying that he or she is "all that sick."

Additionally, remember that a person can have more than one reaction at the same time—for instance, a person may be angry and at the same time depressed. Family members or friends of dying persons also may have multiple reactions. They may be sad or depressed over the death of a parent, but at the same time they may accept the death as the best thing for their loved one.

They may also become frustrated that their loved one "doesn't die." Here's why. When the family has been told their loved one is dying, they go through many different emotions of grief, as we have discussed. When their loved one then rallies, as often happens, they at first are so grateful; however, when this roller coaster of grief continues, they realize that they are going to have to experience those emotions again and again.

There are very few "shoulds" when caring for those who are dying. However, here are a few things to keep in mind:

1. It is important that you continually process with someone your own pain in losing the person to whom you are ministering. You need to tell your story, too! Caregivers who have their own listener are blessed indeed. Often that is a missing element in the process of giving care to the dying.

2. Do not try to produce or force a certain reaction in a dying person or to rush him or her through one stage of grief into another. If a person is angry, listen and empathize with that anger, and then help the person express it and deal with it appropriately.

3. Sit in the tension with the person, walking alongside, listening, caring, praying, and loving.

4. Don't say, "It's going to be okay." I recently had someone close to death tell me how tired he was of people telling him this.

This person knew it would be okay in eternity, but it was not going to be okay in the present, and the platitudes added to his frustration.

5. Be sure the patient has an advanced directive, which includes whether he or she accepts or denies certain medical treatments.

6. Help the patient with unfinished business and personal arrangements. It is extremely crucial that those surrounding the patient help him or her with loss issues: physical, emotional, mental, and social. These issues must be dealt with on the individual's timetable and according to his or her agenda, not the agenda of the caregiver. You as the caregiver may be the one person willing to hear all aspects of a patient's story—fears, frustrations, anger, peace, joy—all of it.

7. Being involved with a terminally ill person invariably means being involved with the family, sometimes a very large extended family. As you minister to all of them, be sensitive to the individual needs and the individual stages of their pain. Some family members may want to discuss death; others may refuse. Walk in the other person's shoes without feeling responsible to solve the other's problems. Don't try to rush the care receiver.

8. Invite the patient and family members to process with you the inappropriate things that they or others are saying, as well as their own fears and anxieties and their frustrations. For example, if you were caring for the dying woman who was told, "Everything is going to be okay," you might reflect on how hard it must be to hear things that are upsetting. If you were talking to the person who said this to her, it might be appropriate to say something like "Sometimes it's difficult to know just the right thing to say, isn't it? I have found that I don't have to have the 'right answers.' I just have to let her know that I care."

9. Be an encourager to the terminally ill person. Listen to the patient express confusion and frustration as he begins to realize limitations. Assure the patient that you are aware of the pain and will continue to walk beside him. Do not judge him. You may be tempted to retaliate with emotion. Don't.

10. If the patient chooses to set goals, cheer her on in the accomplishment of those goals. Remember that God is a God of hope, and it is appropriate to help instill that in those who are terminally ill. For example, a dying young woman asked me if I thought she would be able to play golf in heaven. My response was that, while I wasn't sure whether that specific activity would be available in heaven, I did know that heaven would be far more amazing than our minds can even begin to comprehend. She didn't need a specific answer as much as an assurance of hope and of my presence with her in her wonderings.

11. Allow the terminally ill to say good-bye in his or her own way. To cope with the overwhelming loss of one's own impending death, that person often begins to gradually withdraw from the world. At this point the dying person might begin in his or her own way to say good-bye to friends, relatives, and immediate family. Near the end the person may prefer to be with one or two people who do nothing more than stay quietly at the bedside. It is indeed a privilege to be that person "beside the bed"—the deathbed is a holy place. God wants us to be available, to listen, and to respond appropriately.

12. Remember, *grief takes as long as it takes.* After the death of someone you have given care to, recognize your own need to grieve.

13. Contact the family a few days after the funeral or memorial service concludes to continue appropriate care for them, particularly as the initial shock of grief wears off and the reality of the loss sets in. Have a plan for continued care. For instance, at a recent funeral I attended, the pastor asked

the adult grandchildren if they knew when their grandparents' anniversary date was. He then asked that they not leave Grandpa alone on either that day or Grandma's birthday.

Walking beside others as they journey through "the valley of the shadow of death" (Psalm 23:4) is an honor. We become the Shepherd's helper on this journey, and He guides us and gives us comfort as we comfort others through this process. Paul encouraged us in 2 Corinthians 1:3-4 with these words: "Praise be to the God and Father of our Lord Jesus Christ, the Father of compassion and the God of all comfort, who comforts us in all our troubles, so that we can comfort those in any trouble with the comfort we ourselves have received from God."

As the Time of Death Nears

This information is helpful for caregivers and family members who are keeping vigil.

Signs of Impending Death

1. As death approaches, there will be less interest in eating and drinking. The refusal of food is often an indication that the person is ready to die. Fluid intake may be limited to that which will keep a person's mouth from feeling too dry.

   What you as a caregiver or family member can do: Offer, but do not force, food, fluids, and medications. Pain that has required medication to control may no longer be a problem.

2. Urinary output may decrease in amount and frequency.

   What you as a caregiver or family member can do: Nothing, unless the patient expresses a desire to urinate and cannot. Call hospice or whoever is overseeing care for advice.

3. As the body weakens, the patient will probably sleep more and begin to detach from his or her environment. Attempts to provide comfort may be refused.

   What you as a caregiver or family member can do: Let him or her sleep. Do not feel compelled to wake the person to administer medications or to continue the same physical care routine that you have followed in the past. At this point "being with" is more important than "doing for."

4. The person may be disturbed by "strange" dreams.

   What you as a caregiver or family member can do: As the patient awakens, remind her of the day and time, where she is, and who is present. This is best done in a casual, conversational way.

5. Vision and hearing may become somewhat impaired, and speech may be difficult to understand.

   What you as a caregiver or family member can do: Speak clearly but no more loudly than necessary. Keep the room as light as the patient wishes, even at night. Carry on all conversations as if they can be heard, since hearing is the last of the senses to cease functioning. Many patients are able to talk until minutes before death and are reassured by the exchange of a few words with a loved one.

6. Secretions may collect in the back of the throat and rattle or gurgle as the patient breathes. The person may try to cough up this mucus, and the mouth may become dry and encrusted with secretions.

What you as a caregiver or family member can do: If he or she is trying to cough up secretions and is experiencing choking or vomiting, humidification of the air with a cool-mist vaporizer may help. Otherwise, call hospice or whoever is overseeing care for advice. Here are some other ways to help:

- Cleanse the mouth with swabs dipped in glycerin, mineral oil, or even cool water to help relieve the dryness that occurs with mouth breathing.
- Offer water in small amounts to keep the mouth moist. A straw with one finger placed over the end can be used to transfer sips of water to the patient's mouth.
- Secretions can be drained from the mouth if the patient is placed on his or her side and supported with pillows.

7. Breathing may become irregular with periods of no breathing, or apnea, lasting around twenty to thirty seconds. The patient may seem to be working very hard to breathe and may make a moaning sound with each breath. As the time of death nears, breathing may again become regular, but shallower and more mechanical in nature.

What you as a caregiver or family member can do: Raise the head of the bed if the patient breathes more easily this way. The "moaning" is not necessarily indicative of pain or distress but often is only the sound of air passing over very relaxed vocal cords.

8. As the oxygen supply to the brain decreases, the patient may become restless. It is not unusual for patients to pull at bed linens, to have visual hallucinations, or even to try to get out of bed at this point.

    What you as a caregiver or family member can do: Reassure the patient in a calm voice that you are there. Prevent him from falling if he tries to get out of bed. Soft music or a back rub may help quiet the person.

9. During the dying process, blood circulating to the skin is decreased and causes a number of changes, such as bluish-colored hands and feet, and sweating or perspiration. The skin next to the bed will darken. The pulse may be hard to feel or find.

    What you as a caregiver or family member can do: Provide the patient with a cool washcloth if this promotes comfort. Change perspiration-soaked garments and bed linens if the patient wishes.

10. Loss of control of bladder and bowel function may occur around the time of death.

    What you as a caregiver or family member can do: Protect the mattress with plastic. Keep waterproof padding under the patient, and change as needed to keep the patient comfortable.

At the Time of Death

1. Breathing ceases.
2. Heartbeat ceases.
3. The patient cannot be aroused.
4. The eyelids may be partially open, with the eyes in a fixed stare.
5. The mouth may fall open slightly as the jaw relaxes.
6. Any waste matter in the bladder or rectum will be released as the sphincter muscles relax.

Adapted with permission from Denver Hospice, Denver, Colorado.

Walking a Family Through a Death

If you have been designated as the pastoral caregiver to a family whose loved one is dying, take the following steps as you walk the family through grief.

Upon Notification of Death
1. Contact the family as soon as possible.
2. Offer assistance by utilizing the ABCs of caregiving— (tell them who you are, that you know, that you care): "Hi, this is Barb Roberts. I just learned about the death of your mom, and I am so sorry. I wanted to see what I can do to help." If the death has been sudden, the shock stage will be severe. The care needed in that situation is much more intense.

First Meeting with Family
As soon as possible, meet with the family. (If the meeting is immediately after the death at the hospital, the hospital staff may bring up the possibility of organ donation. This may be a difficult hurdle for family members to have to face, particularly if they have not discussed it before.)

1. In this initial meeting with family members, express your sorrow over their loss and give them a hug or shake their hand. If you knew the person who died, this would be a good time to offer a thought about your own fondness for the person.

   I am always sensitive to how the family members are reacting. Some families will come into this initial meeting "all business"—even in the midst of their grief. They will jump right into planning the funeral or memorial service. In other cases, I might say something like "This has been a rough time for you all" (or "a rough few days" or "a long, difficult journey"—depending on the cause of death and the length of the illness). Often that open-ended statement will help family members open up about their loved one or the dying process.

This meeting may be a good time to say, "Tell me some of your memories about . . ." You may even encourage them to share funny stories. Again, be sensitive to the family members.

2. When there are young children in the family meeting, choose your words carefully. It is not appropriate, for example, to tell the children that Daddy or Grandpa has gone away. (Next time Mommy or Grandma go away, the child will fear that they will not return either.) You might say something simple, like "Daddy is in heaven with Jesus." Even young children can tell when something is wrong within the family. If the child is in the denial stage, it is important to allow him or her to work through this without facing the truth too quickly. Give children the opportunity to participate in the meeting without expecting or forcing their involvement.

3. Help with immediate decision making as you are asked. Do not take over control of the decisions. Remember that often, even when the grieving person asks you to make a very important decision for him or her (for instance, Should I order an autopsy?), that person is not expecting you to decide. People in grief need to express their questions, and you need to be willing to be present to whatever their expressions are.

The family needs to:

- Decide on burial or cremation. You may be asked to give your input if the family has not previously discussed this issue.
- Choose a mortuary (offer to contact a mortician).
- Choose a cemetery (offer to contact a cemetery).
- Choose a pastor (offer to contact a pastor).

4. Share appropriate Scripture if suitable. Consider, for example, Psalm 139:13-18; Psalm 91; and John 14:1-6.
5. Pray with and for the family.

Mortuary Meeting

Offer to accompany family members to the mortuary. Suggest that they bring with them the Social Security number of the deceased and the number of death certificates they will need. (Some mortuaries offer their services at no cost for burial of a child.) Offer as much or as little help as requested regarding:

- Date and time of service
- Decisions about the body
- Burial: casket, viewing, clothing and jewelry
- Cremation: container, disposition
- Entombment
- Notification of other family, friends, and newspapers

Cemetery Meeting

Offer to accompany the family to the cemetery. Prepare the family for the possibility that most often the cemetery requests payment at the time of this meeting (the mortuary is usually willing to bill the family). Offer as much or as little help as requested in regard to:

- Choosing the burial site. (Some cemeteries have designated sections for babies, and there is no charge for the plot.)
- Choosing the vault.
- Choosing the tombstone (this decision may be delayed).

Second Meeting with Family

Sometimes planning the service occurs at the first meeting; other times it may be necessary to have a second meeting to finalize plans for the services. Request the following information from the family and then give it to the pastoral staff to aid them in planning the service.

- Name of spouse or closest relative and phone number
- Names of other family members
- Cause of death

- ❧ Information about the deceased
- ❧ Funeral or memorial (body is present at a funeral and not at a memorial)
- ❧ Name of mortuary and cemetery
- ❧ Viewing or visitation
- ❧ Graveside service
- ❧ Order of service
- ❧ Bulletin
- ❧ Favorite music
- ❧ Favorite Scriptures
- ❧ Names of pallbearers and other friends and family participating in service. Does the family want to share anecdotes and personal stories at the service? Will there be open sharing? An alternative to open sharing at the service is to provide "memory cards" on which the friend can share a brief memory. These cards will be given to the family after the service.
- ❧ Creative touches. Particularly in the funeral for a child, help the family understand that creative touches are appropriate, such as releasing balloons or doves after the service, giving opportunity for expressions that exemplify their loved one. Family members may each be given a special flower to place on the casket or to take with them. It can be helpful for grieving adults and children to write letters about or to their loved one that can then be read at the service by them or someone else. Another wonderful addition to the service might be to display a collage of pictures of the loved one or to have a slideshow, with accompanying music, during the service.
- ❧ Organist, pianist, or other musicians
- ❧ Reception after service
- ❧ Disposition of flowers after service
- ❧ Memorial fund designation

After-Care

1. Call the family two to four days after the services, just to check in.
2. Discuss their grieving process, as appropriate.
3. Ask family members if they would like to have someone to talk to or pray with — perhaps a meeting with the pastor or a leader in the church. It would then be helpful for you as the pastoral caregiver to arrange for that meeting.
4. Talk with the family about joining a grief group, if appropriate.
5. Have a follow-up plan in place to help you remember anniversary dates.

CARING FOR A FAMILY WHEN A CHILD HAS DIED

If you are the pastoral caregiver for a family whose child has died . . .

1. Be available immediately. The death of a child is a parent's worst nightmare. When you hear of the death, clear your schedule and arrange for the care of any other children in the grieving family.

2. Recognize that *all* will be in shock. The shock stage for the parents will be intense, but may be manifested in a variety of ways. Some will be nonfunctional and will need you to help them with immediate decisions. Others will appear to be functioning well and "directing traffic," making decisions right and left. Your tasks may vary, depending on the degree of functionality. Do not assume that both parents are "in the same place" — grief is individual.

3. Be careful not to offer spiritual (or other) platitudes. Be very careful when sharing Scripture at this initial stage. While our comfort does come from God and from His Word, allow Him to guide your use of Scripture. Anger may accompany grief, and that anger may be displaced at God or God's caregiver — you.

4. Offer your loving presence. Do not try to "fix their pain" or answer "why." The family members who have just experienced the death of a child (parents, siblings, grandparents, others) don't need answers. This is the time for a gentle hug, a pat on the shoulder, or an offer to run an errand.

5. You may need to be a behind-the-scenes caregiver, running errands, answering phone calls, taking messages, running the vacuum, preparing meals, helping write thank-you notes — giving very practical help. Pray for and with the adults and with the children as appropriate.

6. Suggest practical steps that must be taken. As it becomes necessary to make final arrangements, refer to "Walking a

Family Through a Death" on pages 71–75 and part 5 on grief. With the death of a child, take this "arrangement process" slowly. Respond to the family's questions rather than pushing a timetable on them.

7. Don't ask questions to satisfy your own curiosity. There is a fine line between being the "information gatherer"—attaining facts that others will need—and asking questions to satisfy your own need for information. The former is helpful; the latter adds to the stress of family members.

8. Help the family find a private place to grieve. This may be a separate room in their home, a consultation room at the hospital, or another place away from others who mean well but may not be in the immediate circle of family and close friends.

9. Keep in mind the physical needs of the family. Offer water to drink to prevent dehydration, simple food if someone feels faint, a cool cloth on the forehead.

10. Watch your words. Be willing to sit with the family in the "tension" of silence. Do not be cheery in their deep loss. This is a time for you to remember the scriptural principle to "rejoice with those who rejoice; mourn with those who mourn" (Romans 12:15).

11. Do not have *any* expectations of family members. They may not be able to be rational, responsible, calm, or even kind.

12. Remember that each parent grieves differently. Family members will most likely be in different places spiritually as well as in the grieving process. One may be grieving the loss of the present ("I lost a child who still needed me to care for him"); the other may be grieving the loss of the future ("I will never get to take him hunting, be at his high school graduation, walk her down the aisle at her wedding").

13. Your role is to care, not only for the parents but also for the children in the family. Young children may feel more comfortable sharing with you than with Mommy or Daddy,

who is "so sad." Do not force your role as caregiver on the children. Be available. Listen through the silences.

There is a high incidence of divorce in parents who have lost a child, so:

1. Encourage the entire family to share the grief process. Often the parents grieve separately from their remaining children.
2. Encourage the entire family to get grief counseling.
3. Do not put a time limit on anyone's grief. Grief takes as long as it takes.
4. Be available, be available, be available—and listen, listen, listen!
5. Share helpful Scriptures (at an appropriate time) including:

> The LORD is close to the brokenhearted and saves those who are crushed in spirit. (Psalm 34:18)

> Jesus said, "Let the little children come to me, and do not hinder them, for the kingdom of heaven belongs to such as these." (Matthew 19:14)

> If any of you lacks wisdom, he should ask God, who gives generously to all without finding fault, and it will be given to him. (James 1:5)

Helpful Information for Parents of Children Dealing with Death

Here are some things parents can do to help their children deal with death:

1. Teach them about death and grief. There are many opportunities for children to experience grief and loss, and it is best not to shield them from these opportunities. For example, when a pet dies, talk with your children about death and the loss they feel. Or you might prepare them for their grandfather's death by reading them a book that talks about the death of a grandpa. Help your children understand God's love for them and for Grandpa.

2. Bereaved children live in two worlds—the world of the bereaved and the world of the nonbereaved—and they try to go back and forth. For example, at home, their family is grieving the loss of Grandma; at school, their friends are playing and having fun. This is confusing and difficult for children to deal with. You need to be aware of this so you don't have unrealistic expectations of your children.

3. Talk openly with them about your own sadness. If a child sees you crying, you might say something like "Sometimes I feel really sad. How about you? It's okay if you have times when you don't feel sad and want to play with your friends, but it's also okay if sometimes you feel sad and need to cry." This gives your child permission to live in both worlds.

4. When a loved one is given a terminal diagnosis, in very simple terms bring your children into the family discussions. Explain what the diagnosis means, without eliminating the concept of hope. Remind them that God is a God of hope. Let them know that the doctors and nurses are helping the loved one be more comfortable.

5. Allow your children to see the dying person. Give them opportunity to take little gifts that they have made—cards,

pictures, poems—to brighten the loved one's room. In fact, encourage them to write notes and draw pictures about and for the dying family member.

6. If the dying person is the other parent, give your kids every assurance of safety and security. (This is a unique opportunity for the caregiver to help the surviving parent make his or her own end-of-life arrangements, preparing for the ongoing care of the children.)

7. When a loved one dies, give your children accurate information. Use concrete language. To tell a child that someone "passed away" means nothing to that child. Instead, tell your children that their loved one died and why. There is usually a precise reason for death. For example, you might say, "Grandpa died because his heart stopped beating."

8. Help your children understand the difference between illness, injury, surgery, or hospitalization and terminal illness. If Grandpa died in the hospital, they may be fearful when Daddy is rushed to the hospital with an emergency appendicitis attack.

9. Answer questions honestly, but on the children's level. This is a good opportunity to remember that wise counsel: "Less is more!" Listen for the meaning behind the words. Answer what your children are really asking, not assuming you know the "real" question.

10. Allow your children to see your display of emotion. Parents, it is okay to cry in front of your kids. In fact, if they do not see you cry, they may not understand that you miss Grandpa too. In addition, as your children watch you grieving and talking openly about it, it helps them deal with their own grief.

11. If your children are angry, do not try to squelch their expressions of anger, even if they are angry with God.

12. If you need time alone, express that in appropriate ways. Make sure your kids are safe and feel safe. Allow others to help you. This is a good time to call on trusted, caring friends to help with childcare.

13. Allow children to attend the funeral or memorial service if they want to. This is a very individual decision. There are no "shoulds." Some families bring along an additional person to care for the children if they need to be taken out of the service.

14. If the children will be at the service, decide ahead of time whether they should view the body. If you wish that they do (and if the kids wish to see the body as well), prepare them for what they will see. For example, you might say something like "While the body you'll see is Grandpa's body, the part of Grandpa that opened his eyes, laughed with you, teased and played with you is in heaven with Jesus. This is just his body, so he will not look exactly as he did before. Grandpa is no longer sick or feeling any pain. He is in heaven with Jesus."

15. Allow children to express their grief in their own way. Listen to your kids without judgment or punishment when they express whatever emotions they are carrying inside. Children may sob at the funeral, and during the reception may be running and laughing. That is the beauty of children, and younger children have a short "grief span." While they need to be taught to be respectful, they do not need to be "adult" in their grief expressions.

16. After the service, talk with your children about their feelings. For example, talk about Grandpa and how they are missing him. If a child was angry with the loved one prior to the death, make sure the child understands he or she did not cause the death.

17. Be sure to include the children in after-funeral family times. Do not "ship the child off" to Uncle Harold's without helping him or her feel loved, safe, and secure.

18. Do not tell a boy he is the "man of the house" if Dad died, or a girl to be the "woman of the house" if Mom died. Do not lay this heavy burden on the shoulders of a young child.

Suicide Warning Signs

There is no typical suicide victim. Suicide happens to young and old, rich and poor. Though there may be certain age groups, ethnic groups, and economic groups who appear to be at higher risk for suicide, it is important for the caregiver not to use those boxes to delay help for someone who is despairing. Fortunately, there are common warning signs that, when acted upon, can save lives.

A person might be suicidal if he or she displays a number of the following behaviors:

1. Talks about committing suicide.
2. Suddenly has trouble eating or sleeping and is despondent, with little interest in "life."
3. Experiences drastic changes in behavior, such as losing all interest in things that have previously been important.
4. Withdraws from friends and social activities.
5. Loses interest in hobbies, work, or school.
6. Prepares for death by making out a will or funeral arrangements, gets affairs in order, and contacts family members and friends to tell them he or she loves them in ways that seem to be saying good-bye.
7. Gives away prized possessions.
8. Has attempted suicide before.
9. Has had recent and severe losses, especially a suicide by someone close.
10. Is preoccupied with death and dying.
11. Loses interest in personal appearance.
12. Dramatically increases use of drugs and alcohol.
13. Suddenly appears euphoric, after having been depressed.
    (Once the decision is made to commit suicide, the person may feel resolute in following through with the plan, and his or her demeanor changes.)

Suicide Threats — What Should You Do?

If someone tells you he or she is considering suicide . . .

Do

1. Take all plans and threats seriously (even if you suspect this is "merely a plea for attention"). You cannot take the risk that you may be wrong.
2. Be direct. Talk openly and matter-of-factly about suicide. Inquire about a suicide plan and the means to carry out that plan. For example, "Are you considering harming yourself?" If the person says yes, follow up with "Do you have a plan?"
3. Be a good listener. Make an open-ended statement, such as "I am so sorry that you hurt so much." Allow expression of feelings and accept those feelings.
4. Help the person understand that the consequences are permanent.
5. Get involved and take action. Remove the *means* by which the person has planned to commit suicide, such as a gun or stock-piled pills.
6. Affirm there is hope. Discuss other difficult times and remind them they have gotten through those times.
7. Set up a plan for help, which includes you as the caregiver having a professional you may call for help. In introducing the help plan to the suicidal person, say something like "We'll go together to talk with . . . " "I will help you sort this out."
8. Get help from hotlines or agencies (Boys Town National Hotline — 1-800-448-3000 — or National Suicide Prevention — 1-800-273-8255).
9. Ask the person to tell his or her parents, spouse, best friends, and so on. (If the person is underage, call the parents.) Have the person make the call right then. Tell the person if he or she refuses, you must alert family members and friends, because the person's safety is very important to you.

10. Have the person commit to call you first (make sure he or she has your number) if seriously contemplating suicide. You must be available 24/7.

Don't

1. Don't dare the person to follow through on his or her threat.
2. Don't act shocked with what the person tells you. This will put a distance between you.
3. Don't be sworn to secrecy.
4. Don't be judgmental.
5. Don't debate, either about the issues involved or the need to get help. It is better to have a person angry with you, the caregiver, than to have him or her dead.

Helpful Information for Those Who Lose Someone to Suicide

The following information can help those who have lost someone to suicide recognize God's available presence, love, and power.

1. Recognize that you are in shock. Shock is a first reaction to death, particularly death by suicide.
2. Acknowledge that you are grieving. It is common to experience physical reactions to grief, such as headaches, loss of appetite, and an inability to sleep. You may also feel angry, guilty, confused, and forgetful. You may feel overwhelmed by the intensity of your feelings, but know that all your feelings are normal. At times your grief and sadness will surface very strongly. *You are not crazy; you are in mourning.*
3. Understand that guilt — "if only" — is perhaps the most intense emotion you will struggle with. You may have sensed the possibility of suicide, but you thought your loved one was "getting better." It is common for a suicidal person to feel better once the decision to die has been made.
4. Expressing anger with the person who committed suicide, with the world, with God, with yourself is appropriate and okay. If you are angry with God, share that anger with a godly, trustworthy person.
5. Call someone if you need to talk; tell your story as often as you need to. If your friends seem uncomfortable talking about the death, choose a few people close to you with whom you can share your story. For others, only discuss those parts of your story that you feel comfortable sharing.
6. Take one moment or one day at a time.
7. Don't be afraid to cry. Tears are healing.
8. Give yourself time to heal; grief takes as long as it takes.
9. Try to put off major decisions.
10. Give yourself permission to get professional help.

11. Be aware of the pain of your family and friends. You are not the only one suffering.

12. Be patient with yourself and with others who may not understand.

13. Set your own limits and learn to say no.

14. Know that there are support groups that can be helpful, such as Compassionate Friends or Survivors of Suicide groups. If such a group is not available in your area, ask a professional to help start one.

15. Call on your personal faith to help you through.

16. Be willing to laugh with others, and at yourself; it is healing.

17. Letting go doesn't mean forgetting. Have people in your life with whom you can share memories, thoughts, and anecdotes of your loved one.

18. Understand that your life will not return to "normal," but you can survive and even go beyond just surviving. You now have a new "normal" in your life and in the life of your family.

Helping Staff Members, Congregations, and Student Bodies Deal with Death, Including Suicide

Pastoral caregivers can help during the first few weeks following a death in the following ways:

1. Be watchful for contagion, guilt, and modeling—particularly with suicides.
2. Do not glorify the situation, especially a suicide.
3. Do not deny or ignore the situation, even during the funeral or memorial service.
4. Allow for fatigue for survivors and caregivers. Stress, grief, and a loss of control can be exhausting.
5. Realize that emotional reactions vary in nature and intensity. Try to be open to changing moods and feelings—shock, anxiety, horror, fear, guilt, and depression—saying something like "This must be a terrible shock for you." The person has the opportunity to respond with "yes" or "no," but it gets the conversation started.
6. Knowing what to say is often difficult. It is usually sufficient to give a hug and say, "This is really hard for us." It helps people remember they are not alone.
7. Set up times for all staff members and volunteers to discuss, process, and pray. Be sure to include all those who were involved with the person on committees or small groups, including all who were impacted.
8. Send a letter to each person involved in the life of the deceased, emphasizing the need to support each other, giving factual information, and announcing support meeting times and places.
9. Continue to be aware of the need to be mutually supportive.
10. Encourage those who were personally involved with someone who died or was injured to attend discussion times. Identify a specific person to be supportive to that individual for the first two weeks.

11. Make ongoing pastoral care or mental health support available.

12. Be honest with people, including children and adolescents, about what is happening and about your own grief and loss.

13. Help those who are not good with words, including children and adolescents, with terminology and vocabulary that helps them express deeper feelings. For instance, you might say, "It seems to me that you're feeling (confused, angry, sad) about this." Allow them time to reflect back to you whether your suggested words represent what they are feeling.

14. Be aware that some people will not cry or exhibit sadness but will instead act out or become angry. Usually a few words of understanding will soothe these feelings. Do not be judgmental about how people express grief.

15. Watch for these distress signals from those who are particularly impacted; for example, best friends or siblings of adolescents:

   - Changes in eating or sleeping habits that persist over two weeks.
   - Severe mood swings.
   - Significantly decreased interest in work, family, and friends.
   - Isolating oneself from family and friends.
   - Hopelessness.
   - A plan of action or thinking about suicide. Ask directly! Refer to a professional mental-health agency or individual immediately.
   - Be especially aware of those who have a previous history of suicide ideation, attempts, or risk-taking behaviors.

Adapted from materials written by Ruth Gonzalez, PhD, psychologist, Lewis and Clark College, Portland, Oregon.

CARING FOR SURVIVORS OF SUDDEN INFANT DEATH SYNDROME (SIDS)

If you are caring for SIDS survivors:

1. Go as soon as you receive the call.
2. Don't try to have the perfect thing to say. A hug and "I'm so sorry" are enough.
3. Listen to the information the parents choose to give you. Don't pump them with questions to satisfy your curiosity.
4. Be the silent presence in the background, helping to bring order out of chaos.
5. Offer to handle practical details, such as making phone calls, walking with them through the funeral planning (see "Walking a Family Through a Death" on pages 71–75 and part 5, "Grief"), and arranging for meals to be brought to their home. (Another helpful section for the caregiver is "Dos and Don'ts in Grief Care" on pages 113–114.)
6. Be what the parents need you to be. If they need to talk about what happened, listen compassionately and empathetically. If they need your silent presence, be available for them. I have experienced being in the mortuary with parents in the presence of the baby in an open casket. At times during the visitation, they held their baby. They needed me to be with them as a quiet, prayerful presence.
7. Your emotions may be intense through the caregiving process—as you talk with the parents, as you view the baby, as you think of your own child or grandchild, or as you help the parents pick out the casket. Ask the Holy Spirit to be *your* Comforter. If the parents ask if you want to hold the child, that is your decision as a caregiver. There are no "shoulds"!
8. Talk with others in the family who are hurting—grandparents, siblings, other family members, and close friends. Ask what you can do for them, such as offering to make phone

calls, listening to their own story, praying with them.

9. Make sure you do follow-up care. Call, visit (calling first), send cards, arrange meals. Remember the baby's birthday, date of death, Mother's Day, and Father's Day.

HELPFUL INFORMATION FOR PARENTS WHO HAVE LOST A CHILD THROUGH SIDS

The following information is helpful to those who have lost a child through SIDS. It encourages them to recognize God's available presence, love, and power.

1. Allow others to share your grief and to walk beside you through this "valley of the shadow of death." You are not to blame. Pour out your heart to God—your hurt, your pain, your anger.
2. Share your grief with your spouse, even if he or she is in a different place than you are.
3. Recognize that grief is a process and takes as long as it takes. Care for yourself and allow others to care for you. If you have other children, care for them and allow them to share in your grief. They are hurting too.
4. Meditate on Scripture that may be helpful to you. Here are a few passages:

> The righteous cry out, and the Lord hears them;
>   he delivers them from all their troubles.
> The LORD is close to the brokenhearted
>   and saves those who are crushed in spirit.
> A righteous man may have many troubles,
>   but the LORD delivers him from them all.
>   (Psalm 34:17-19)

> God is our refuge and strength,
>   an ever-present help in trouble.
> Therefore we will not fear, though the earth give way
>   and the mountains fall into the heart of the sea,

though its waters roar and foam
    and the mountains quake with their surging.
        (Psalm 46:1-3)

For you created my inmost being;
    you knit me together in my mother's womb.
I praise you because I am fearfully and wonderfully made;
    your works are wonderful,
    I know that full well.
My frame was not hidden from you
    when I was made in the secret place.
When I was woven together in the depths of the earth,
    your eyes saw my unformed body.
All the days ordained for me
    were written in your book
    before one of them came to be. (Psalm 139:13-16)

When you pass through the waters,
    I will be with you;
and when you pass through the rivers,
    they will not sweep over you.
When you walk through the fire,
    you will not be burned;
    the flames will not set you ablaze.
For I am the LORD, your God . . .
Since you are precious and honored in my sight,
    and because I love you . . . " (Isaiah 43:2-4)

CARING FOR COUPLES EXPERIENCING INFERTILITY, MISCARRIAGE, OR INFANT LOSS

The following recommendations come out of Marie Foote's personal experience with loss. Please do not expect every couple you help to want every single thing in this list.

When the Lord led my husband, Jordan, and me onto the path of multiple miscarriages over six years ago, we learned a tremendous amount about grief, pain, suffering, anger, sadness, bitterness, jealousy, and disappointment. He also taught us valuable truths about healing, trust, friendship, provision, acceptance, surrender, and joy.

Do

1. *Say something to acknowledge their loss.* I heard so many times that my friends did not want to say anything to make our situation worse, so they said nothing at all. I appreciated their desire not to make a bad situation worse, but it made it much worse that they never acknowledged my pain. Remember this: Any discomfort you feel from the awkwardness of the situation will never equal the hurt inflicted by the loss itself. You do not have to say much to communicate that you are sad and that you care. Profound words are not a requirement for extending a healing hand in friendship and concern.

2. *Ask the couple if they are comfortable with your calling or visiting on a regular basis.* If the answer is yes, ask when is a good time, then do your best to communicate your intentions in advance so they can prepare themselves for your call or visit. There were some days when my outlook was brightened by the mere anticipation of a friend or family member's visit or phone call, and there were days when I did not want to see, be seen by, or talk to anyone. You will never know what kind of day the couple is having unless you ask.

3. *When you call, ask, "Is this a good time to talk?"* It is considerate to give people an out if now is not a good time. You want

and need to be there for them, but it's good to have it be on their own terms and comfort level. If it's not, there may not be much benefit from your time and effort.

4. *Arrange for meals to be brought to the family for at least three weeks after the death.* Grief is draining. The distraction of meal preparation may be energizing for some couples during their time of sorrow, but for us, it was nice to have one less thing to do. It's a simple but tangible way to acknowledge that this time is difficult and that you are available to serve them.

5. *Make your home available to them, if you are able to do so.* Sometimes my husband and I felt the need to get out of our house, but the thought of being in a busy restaurant or a crowded mall was overwhelming for us. Even being at church was extremely painful. When friends and family invited us over to their home for a few hours, it felt like we were "getting away," but we did not have to put as much effort into it because we could go just as we were. Don't be offended if the couple says no. Sometimes the invitation can be encouragement enough, and they may take you up on it at some point, when they are ready.

6. *Make an effort to pray* with *the couple, instead of only praying for* them. It always ministered to me to have people talk to the God of the universe about my pain, in my presence. After our first miscarriage, one couple came to our house every week and prayed with us, that God would grant us a child. Even though their prayers were for a healthy pregnancy and God chose not to give us that, we learned much from this couple about the role of faith and hope in prayer. Another way to pray with a couple is to write out your prayer for them so they have it in writing and can read it anytime they have a need for it.

7. *Organize a prayer meeting for the couple.* Some friends gathered one night to lift my husband and me up before the Lord. Even though we chose not to go (we did not have the energy to walk out the door), it soothed our spirits to know that people cared

enough to set aside time, on a night when they could have chosen to do so many other things, and pray for God to be with us.

8. *Write cards or e-mails, or leave phone messages if you are not able to connect in person.* We have kept every encouraging card and e-mail sent to us since we lost our twins six years ago. I saved encouraging phone messages for months after they were left on our voicemail. We see those as a testament of God's great provision in our lives. Those moments of contact from the outside world carried us through some dark days. Never hesitate to obey if the Spirit prompts you to reach out with a note or a call.

9. *Remember the due date and anniversary of the loss.* This is particularly important for the first year, but even in the years after, especially if the family still expresses feelings about it when you ask. For couples who struggle with infertility, when there is no due date or anniversary of a death, the anniversary of when they began attempting or desiring pregnancy is often a painful time. Ask them when that date falls, and if they tell you, write them a card or give them a little gift acknowledging your ongoing, loving concern and prayer for them. I am blessed to have thoughtful friends who still verbalize to me that they know the autumn season ushers in some feelings of sadness and melancholy for me because I miscarried three babies between the months of October and December.

Remember, too, that couples in intense grief often feel the loneliest during the holidays, a time when all the world seems so happy around them. Mother's Day, Father's Day, and Sanctity of Human Life Day can all be painful Sundays, even long after the couple has begun to experience healing from their grief. It is generally a good time to connect with them and to remind them that you are thinking of them and that you have not forgotten the holes in their hearts.

10. *Use the child's name if the couple does.* If the couple has chosen to name their child, your use of the name validates the reality of the child's life and death. On the other hand, if a couple chooses not to name their child, defer to the term the couple uses (baby, boy, girl, and so on). I took great comfort in hearing people use my babies' names, but I also had friends who miscarried who chose to call their child "my baby." I realized that healing power wasn't in the specific name of the child, but in my friends' and family's willingness to join me in my grief by identifying with yet another aspect of my grieving heart.

11. *Be intentional about your ministry to the couple.* Communicate with them all along the way. Take your cues from the couple, and be willing to let the Holy Spirit change your plans if He impresses you to do or say something different. For example, one couple I knew seemed eager to talk about their miscarriage in the beginning. As the weeks stretched into months, my occasional questions about how they were doing seemed to be met with shrugs and evasion. At one point, I felt that the wife was showing annoyance with me and that her replies seemed more and more clipped. I wasn't sure what to do, because I had promised to check in with them occasionally. The Lord led me to ask them one last time how they were doing. I made sure I communicated my willingness to be available again, just as I had promised, but that if they no longer wanted to talk, I would no longer ask them how they were doing unless they brought it up. I never heard from them after that until they reentered the world happily one day, announcing that they were expecting once again. After that news, it made sense to me that their withdrawal had been related to their new pregnancy. They did not dare announce it to everyone yet, so they were, in a sense, trapped between their new secret joy and their fear of the way their last pregnancy had ended.

12. *Apologize genuinely if it comes to your attention that you may have been hurtful in any way.* Not too long ago, a friend who has struggled with infertility for years expressed to me her feelings that I had neglected her and "moved on" because I was now the mother of two children. (Those who are grieving often need to be pursued, and sometimes their hurt feelings do not come out right away, particularly if they are not outgoing or outspoken people.) While my friend's accusation about my motive was, in my mind, untrue, I recognized that she was feeling intense pain and disappointment that yet another year had gone by and she was still childless.

    As I prayed about how to handle the situation, the Lord impressed upon me to offer a simple apology and explanation of how I felt about our friendship. There was no need to present a defense of my every action. What she needed to hear was that I still wanted her in my life. What needed to be resolved were her feelings of being abandoned by me. She was the one who was hurting deeply. I needed to defer to her feelings.

13. *Forgive them if they hurt you.* A person who is hurting deeply is eventually bound to say or do something offensive to someone. I never wanted to hurt anyone when I was in grief, but sometimes I did so because my pain made me more myopic than usual. Pain can make us more self-centered, unfortunately. Be assured that most grieving people will not remain in that state forever. Healing will come one day, and you will be a better person for practicing forbearance.

14. *Remember that every person, every couple, grieves in different ways.* There is no appropriate length of time before a grieving person or couple should have "moved on" from their pain. Everyone travels this road at a different pace. No one follows the same pattern or timeline, because we have all been created as unique individuals. Be patient and gracious, even when it becomes tiresome.

15. *Use Scripture, but use it wisely.* There were times when, right or wrong, I perceived that people were quoting Scripture to help me "buck up" and "move on" with my life. Used appropriately, God's Word will breathe life into a dying heart. A wounded person can sense when you're using Scripture to encourage him and when you're doing it because you hope it will get him out of his pity party. Imagine that any verses you would offer a hurting couple have been stamped by the Holy Spirit, "Proceed with caution, and only with my permission."

16. *Recognize that you may not be the best person to help the couple.* If you sense that you may not be the one to be the "hands-on" caregiver, I have found that the best way to avoid making the wrong assumption about what the couple wants and needs is to *ask* them openly and gently, then be ready to honor what they ask, if it is within reason and within my power to do so. If it becomes clear, after several attempts, that I am not the person to help a couple, I limit my ministry to prayer and ask God to quicken my heart to anything else I can do that would help them. While I was in mourning, though I wanted to hear that people did care, I did not have it in me to pour out my deepest feelings to everyone who was willing to help. There is no logical explanation for who feels safe enough to share with and who doesn't.

17. *Give of yourself, but also set a boundary around your time and your family.* You will burn out if you do not allow yourself some appropriate space from their grief. If you burn out, you will become increasingly frustrated with those you are caring for (and that may come through in your tone of voice!). They also need the space to listen to God's voice, to pull together as a couple, and to figure some things out on their own.

Don't

1. *Don't be afraid to show emotion.* Scripture commands us to rejoice with those who rejoice, but also to mourn with those who mourn (see Romans 12:15). Showing emotion will not prove you weak; it will give the couple strength, knowing that they are not alone in their sadness.

2. *Don't make it about* your *pain.* Focus on the hurting couple and their perspective, especially if it's close to the time of loss. I remember one time when a friend stopped by and began to cry as we talked. I thought for a moment that she was crying for me and my loss, then she said, "You just lost a baby, another friend just lost her babies—I am afraid that I will be next." While I wanted to comfort her because she was obviously in distress, I also wanted to scream at her, "You have healthy, beautiful children. What are you crying about?"

3. *Don't offer any comfort with the words,* "Well, at least . . ." Anything that follows those words serves only one purpose: minimizing their pain. The first friend that I spoke to after we lost our twins said, "Well, at least you know you can get pregnant easily." In retrospect and after grief counseling, I know now she meant to communicate that she felt hopeful about my future as a mother; however, those words stung my heart for months.

   Let the couple come to these kinds of conclusions themselves (God will guide them in His way and His time), and affirm those truths when the couple chooses to verbalize them to you. For example, if the couple says, "We feel better knowing our son is in a better place," you can affirm their conclusion, saying, "Yes, I'm grateful for that too. I can imagine that it really hurts that you don't have him in your arms as well." That communicates comfort and hope much better than, "Well, honey, at least your son is in a better place." Often, all the couple needs to hear is that you know they are hurting and you hurt with them. They know you don't have the answers as to why they are infertile or why their baby died.

4. *Don't disappear after a few weeks.* Keep coming back and checking in with them, no matter how pointless it may seem to you. The most difficult time in a crisis is not the first month, when numbness and shock are still in play and when people flock to the aid of the grieving. The second, third, and fourth months—when everyone has seemingly gone back to "life as usual"—is when the numbness wears off and when the pain sets in with intensity. Unfortunately, this is when support is most needed and most difficult to find.

Because my husband's and my initial grief event repeated itself in subsequent miscarriages, we did eventually experience people throwing their hands up in the air, not because they didn't care for us, but because it just went on for so long and they did not know what to do with us anymore. Only those who stayed the course with us truly saw God do His mightiest work in our hearts. Consider all things carefully before you choose to release a couple only to God's care.

5. *Don't tell them not to be angry.* In fact, never tell them how to feel. People in grief can control their feelings as much as you can control the weather. When people told me not to be angry, it only served to fuel my anger at their inability to understand my heart—someone who was a follower of Jesus, but who was also hurting intensely. When I expressed doubts, questions, or anger, it wasn't because I had forsaken my relationship with Christ. I was wrestling with Him because I wanted to reconcile my pain and shattered dreams with my trust in His sovereignty.

6. *Don't judge them for being angry and expressing doubt.* Some of the most compassionate friends I had during our darkest days were people who had never, ever had a moment of struggle with pregnancy and childbearing, but I did experience judgment from those who had experienced what I had. One friend

tried so hard to get me to accept my losses long before I was ready, simply because she had come to that place much more quickly than I had. She admitted at one point that her motivation for being insistent with me was that she did not want me to stop walking with Jesus. While I appreciated her concern, it saddened me that she took my doubts, questions, and anger to mean that I was no longer walking with Jesus. She completely missed who I was as a person during that time.

7. *Don't overgeneralize and project other people's "success stories" into a situation.* It can be encouraging for a couple to hear that they are not alone in their pain, but sweeping statements about how "lots of people take years to conceive healthy babies before popping them out in record time" or how your Aunt Susie "had ten miscarriages before she had quintuplets" may not have the intended effect. To them, Aunt Susie and those "lots of other people" have nothing to do with this event.

8. *Don't give up on them.* Healing takes time. You may find yourself frustrated for, or even with, a sad or angry couple, but their eventual healing is not up to you. All you can really do is love them the best way you know how, make a sincere effort to express your care, pray consistently, and leave the results for their heart journey to God.

Adapted with permission from Marie Foote, Denver, Colorado.

Helping Families Cope with a Violent Death

In your role as a caregiver, you may come alongside a family who has lost a loved one in a violent death.

1. Serve as a prayerful, caring listener. Recognize that the trauma of a violent death exacerbates the grieving process, both the length of time it takes to stabilize and the intensity of the emotions.

2. Your role as caregiver will be intensified as well. In addition to caring for the family, you may have to deal with numerous distractions, such as reporters and curiosity seekers.

3. Help the family appoint someone to deal with the media — whether it is you or a trusted family friend.

4. Help the family understand that one of God's gifts at the time of tragedy is a "covering of shock," which allows people to move into autopilot mode, dealing with initial arrangements. Once the initial shock subsides, the immensity of the loss may envelop them, and your role as caregiver will be even more significant.

5. Be in tune with the roller coaster of emotions and be available to hear the day-to-day stories. You must be committed for the duration — through the police reports, a trial, or whatever involvements may be needed.

6. Encourage family members to talk with others who have gone through traumatic loss. While such people may not know exactly how each person is feeling at any given moment, they definitely can understand the pain more than others who have not experienced the violent death of a loved one.

7. Help family members understand that many will tell them to "just keep busy," but it's important that they don't keep so busy that they fail to take the time needed to grieve and to experience and express their feelings — whether they feel anger, frustration, or deep sorrow.

8. Encourage individual and family counseling for survivors of violent death.

9. Caution the family not to dull their pain with chemical substances, either drugs or alcohol. They need to feel what they are feeling, as painful as it is. This is part of the healing journey.

10. Encourage the survivors to surround themselves with people who bring comfort, prayer, and a listening ear.

11. Share Scriptures that may be helpful to the family:

> Praise be to the God and Father of our Lord Jesus Christ, the Father of compassion and the God of all comfort, who comforts us in all our troubles, so that we can comfort those in any trouble with the comfort we ourselves have received from God. For just as the sufferings of Christ flow over into our lives, so also through Christ our comfort overflows. (2 Corinthians 1:3-5)

> In the LORD I take refuge.
>   How then can you say to me:
>   "Flee like a bird to your mountain.
> For look, the wicked bend their bows;
>   they set their arrows against the strings
> to shoot from the shadows
>   at the upright in heart.
> When the foundations are being destroyed,
>   what can the righteous do?"
> The LORD is in his holy temple;
>   the LORD is on his heavenly throne.
> He observes the sons of men;
>   his eyes examine them.
> The LORD examines the righteous,
>   but the wicked and those who love violence

his soul hates.
On the wicked he will rain
fiery coals and burning sulfur;
a scorching wind will be their lot.
For the LORD is righteous,
he loves justice;
upright men will see his face. (Psalm 11:1-7)

We need have no fear of someone who loves us perfectly;
his perfect love for us eliminates all dread of what he
might do to us. If we are afraid, it is for fear of what
he might do to us and shows that we are not fully
convinced that he really loves us. (1 John 4:18, TLB)

PART 5

Grief

Come to me, all you who are weary and burdened,
and I will give you rest.
MATTHEW 11:28

MINISTERING THROUGH GRIEF

Every day we experience losses, changes, and transitions we must grieve. Grief is intense emotional suffering caused by loss, and while it is normal, it involves hard work. Grief often begins with shock, whether it involves loss of life, loss of relationship, loss of livelihood, loss of the person's living situation, or loss of health. There may be emotional or physical symptoms as well. Some people openly express their grief; others show no emotion. Those who have lost someone close need time to rest and a person with whom they can express their grief.

Always remember that grief and mourning take as long as they take. The length of the grieving process is as variable as the number of people who experience it. It often depends on the nature of the attachment, the willingness of those grieving to "work" on their grief, and the willingness of family members and friends to give each other permission to grieve and to accept that there is no shortcut to working through the process of grief. We probably don't ever "recover" from grief; instead, we learn to manage and cope.

In the past, the model for Christians was to keep a stiff upper lip and to endure the pain and agony of the loss with little or no expression of emotion. Perhaps even more incongruent with the truth of Scripture are Christians who put on a "happy face," denying the pain of grief, which in effect denies the need for a Savior and a Comforter. Many Christians now recognize that grief does not express a lack of faith in God; instead it can lead us to a deeper understanding of our need for God. Grief is the proper expression of feelings associated with the loss of someone or something significant in our lives.

Many people feel uncomfortable with other people's pain and don't know what to say to those in grief. The more comfortable you are with grief as a natural process, the better able you will be to accept grieving people right where they are and effectively minister to them.

Helpful Things to Say to People Who Are Grieving

The following statements and questions may be encouraging to those who are grieving:

- ❧ I am very sad to hear about your loss.
- ❧ I wish I could take your pain away.
- ❧ I don't know what to say to you, but I do care about you very much.
- ❧ How are you doing at this moment?
- ❧ I entrust you to the only One who can heal you, in time.
- ❧ I don't understand why this has happened to you. I am asking God to heal you and to show you His hand in all this.
- ❧ I hope I can encourage you in some way, maybe not today or tomorrow, but I pray that at some point, I can.
- ❧ I understand if I do not hear from you. Please don't feel like you have to respond to me anytime soon.
- ❧ Take your time. I am here.
- ❧ Thank you for trusting me with your feelings.
- ❧ I care about what you are going through.
- ❧ What may I do to help you get through today?
- ❧ Is there someplace where I may take you today or another day this week?
- ❧ I've never been where you are, but I can imagine you are in incredible pain right now.
- ❧ How may I pray for you today?
- ❧ I have not forgotten you.
- ❧ I miss you.
- ❧ I love you.

Used with permission from Marie Foote, Denver, Colorado.

Helping Children Who Grieve

Children in crisis do not grieve in an orderly and predictable way. One teen said this about how teens view the grief process:

> We listen to you adults talking about the stages of grief, but the way we feel and talk about our grief can change from day to day. Sometimes, when you don't understand teens, you say that we are in "such-and-such a stage." But it's just not that simple! When you hang onto some strict idea about these "stages" you talk about, you don't really help us at all. In fact, it seems like you want to get us to some other stage or something. Why can't you just let us be where we are? I guess we need to remind you that no two of us are alike; each of us is different and special, even if we come from the same family.

Another teen observed, "If you try to push me into the stage you think I should be in, I probably won't like you very much. Maybe you could just follow my lead and let me teach you where I am in my grief. Yeah, that would be kind of nice, if you could just accept me where I am."

Helping troubled teens in crisis is emotionally draining, and caregivers working in this situation need to have their own emotional needs met.

It is important to recognize that when a child isn't expressing his or her emotions, it doesn't mean the feelings are absent. If a child is old enough to love, that child is old enough to grieve. It is imperative that adults know and remember to encourage kids to express their feelings. It's also important not to push kids to do things prematurely. For instance, people often push a child into the Big Man/Big Woman syndrome by expecting him or her to take over for an absent parent. A child, even a teen, is none of these things; and if we expect a child to take on one of these roles, we will cause that child much future frustration and trauma.

When helping children in crisis, it's important not to minimize that crisis. A child who has lost a pet may struggle through some of the same grief issues as an adult who has lost a spouse. Helping that child requires spending time with the child, listening, showing concern, and walking alongside the child. As you care for children who are grieving, remember the words of Jesus when He encouraged His disciples to allow the little children to come to Him, "for the kingdom of God belongs to such as these" (Mark 10:14).

SYMPTOMS OF "NORMAL" GRIEF

The following behaviors are a normal and healthy part of grief:

- ❧ Crying
- ❧ Shock and numbness
- ❧ Repeatedly reviewing the events leading up to death
- ❧ Hallucinations: seeing and hearing things
- ❧ Nightmares
- ❧ Anger, guilt, irritability
- ❧ Apathy and withdrawal
- ❧ Chest pain, abdominal distress, headaches
- ❧ Sense of deceased's presence
- ❧ Sleeplessness
- ❧ Loss of appetite
- ❧ Idealization: "The loved one . . . the relationship . . . was perfect!"
- ❧ Identification with the deceased (for example, wishing to go to heaven too)
- ❧ Hostility

SYMPTOMS OF ATYPICAL GRIEF

The following behaviors indicate atypical grief. If several of these are present, the caregiver should refer the person to a professional counselor.

- ❦ Prolonged grief—The person has made no movement toward resuming some normal life activities after the first year; the person is emotionally stuck in the same place.
- ❦ Delayed recognition of bereavement—There is no expression of grief after death for two weeks or more.
- ❦ Severe depression with insomnia, feelings of unworthiness, great tension, bitter self-reproach, and a need for punishment—The presence of these symptoms may indicate the person is suicidal.
- ❦ A recognized medical disease of a psychosomatic nature, such as ulcerative colitis, rheumatoid arthritis, and asthma or bouts of shaking, breathless attacks, and so on.
- ❦ Hypochondria—The bereaved believes he or she is developing symptoms suffered by the deceased.
- ❦ Overactivity—The bereaved goes into a fury of atypical activity.
- ❦ Furious hostility against specific people.
- ❦ Behavior that is not in accord with the bereaved person's normal social or economic existence.
- ❦ The persistent lack of initiative or drive—The bereaved person is immobilized for a prolonged period.
- ❦ Lack of emotional expression; very little affect in facial expressions.
- ❦ Sudden change from distress to contentment over a short time—This may indicate suicidal tendencies.
- ❦ Preoccupation with suicide—The person talks about joining the deceased, ending it all. If this behavior is present, the caregiver needs to directly ask the person if he or she is considering

suicide. A second question is, "Do you have a suicide plan?" If the answer to either of these is yes, the caregiver needs to take action and encourage the person to get help. If the person refuses, the caregiver needs to intervene by getting family involved, as well as medical or mental health professionals.

Dos and Don'ts in Grief Care

When you are caring for someone who has lost a loved one . . .

Do

1. Get in touch with the person suffering the loss. So often we intend to call, send a card, or bake a pie, and then life happens, and we fail to do so. Thinking about reaching out *doesn't count*! Reach out!

2. Focus on the feelings of the grieving person and realize that just being there is far more valuable than words.

3. Allow those in pain to grieve, in their own way, at their own pace. If you're not comfortable with tears, ask God for help. Recognize that the One who walks with us "through the valley of the shadow of death" will also help us get safely to the other side.

4. Listen. The grieving person needs to talk about the loved one. Ask open-ended questions, giving the person an opportunity to tell as many details as he or she is comfortable sharing with you.

5. Pray for and with the person.

6. Talk about the deceased. For example, say things like "Your father was a fine man. I will miss him."

7. Remember you are a vital part of the grieving person's support system. Never underestimate your role as a caregiver.

8. Remember special holidays with a card, a flower, a phone call, or a visit.

9. Ask when the most difficult time of the day is for them. For some it's morning; for others evening; for others it's going to bed alone. Let them share that pain with you. Once you are aware of their most difficult time of day, pray for them or call them at that time.

10. Include the entire family in your caregiving whenever possible—grandparents, siblings, other family members, and close friends. They are hurting too!

11. Remember that it is not your job to eliminate pain.

Don't

1. Don't say, "I know just how you feel." Even if you have gone through a similar sorrow, you do *not* know how other people feel because you are not them. Your pain is not their pain. Your situation is not theirs. Instead, say something like "I cannot know what you are feeling right now, but I am sorry. Are you overwhelmed?"

2. Don't change the subject when you become uncomfortable. Again, this is about the person in need, not about what makes you comfortable.

3. Don't try to answer why the loss occurred. Be honest and say you do not understand why.

4. Don't put a time frame on the grieving process. *Grief takes as long as it takes.*

5. Don't minimize the loss, no matter what it may be. For example, don't tell a woman who has just miscarried, "Just remember you have plenty of time for other babies," or a family whose loved one suffered over a long period, "It's really a blessing that your dad is no longer suffering, isn't it?" While in the long run that may be true, the reality is that grief is painful.

6. Don't wait until you can think of the perfect thing to say. Just say, "I'm so sorry." The person who grieves wants to know that the loved one is remembered. A hug, a handshake, a tear may be just what is needed.

7. You cannot compare pain, so don't try. Don't tell your own story; instead focus on the one to whom you are giving care.

8. Don't push and ask questions just to satisfy your own curiosity. This is about them, not you.

9. Avoid clichés, trite statements, or euphemisms, such as "God will not give you more than you can handle." While this may be true, it's not the time for such statements. They are not helpful for the one who is suffering.

Dos and Don'ts When Caring for the Newly Widowed

When you are caring for someone who is newly widowed . . .

Do

1. Acknowledge the death with a card or letter. Letters can be saved and read time and again. Share an incident, story, or qualities you appreciated about the deceased.
2. Call to express your love and care. Offer to stop by, remembering that your presence and your contacts mean you care.
3. Ask about practical things that may be needed; the person may have difficulty asking for help. For instance, ask about the need for childcare, meals, phone calls to be made, or errands to be run. If you can't do all the tasks that need to be accomplished, find a resource person to get the needed help.
4. Find out which is the most difficult day of the week or the most difficult time of day for him or her. Pray specifically during those times, and let the person know you are doing so. A significant letdown occurs after the funeral, when friends have returned to their own routines, and this will let the grieving spouse know that you care and are interceding for him or her.
5. Remember that the grieving person wants to talk, even though he or she may cry. *Be comfortable with tears*, wait patiently, and encourage the person to tell his or her story.
6. Invite the widowed to your home for dinner. He or she usually doesn't eat well and may long for a home-cooked meal.
7. Invite the widowed to accompany you to concerts, movies, the theater, to play golf, or to participate in whatever activities may be appropriate.
8. Include your widowed friend as before — in dinner parties, on your Christmas card list, in gatherings that previously included them as a couple, such as your Bible study or small group.

9. Frequently ask how you might be praying specifically for and with the person.

Don't

1. Don't say, "I know just how you feel." Even if you also have experienced a death, you don't know how the other person feels. Instead say something like "I cannot know what you feel right now, but I am sorry."
2. Don't be afraid to mention the name of the deceased. The widowed person wants to talk about someone who has been a very important part of his or her life. Tell the grieving spouse you miss the loved one too. Reminisce together.
3. Don't try to "fix" his or her pain.
4. Don't give false encouragement, saying things like "You are so strong!" or "You seem to be doing so well!"
5. Don't give up on the person, even if he or she is moody.
6. Don't mention remarriage. Don't say things like "You're young; you will marry again." Such comments discount the life of the deceased partner and are not appreciated by a grieving spouse. On the other hand, don't be critical or judgmental when the person begins dating.
7. Don't assign the role of the deceased parent to the eldest son or daughter. Don't say, "Now you're the man [or woman] of the house." Such responsibility burdens a young person with an impossible task.

Helpful Information for the Recently Widowed

The following information can be shared with those who have recently lost a spouse. Encourage and support them in these areas:

1. Recognize that while some days will be better than others, you will never get "over it." There is no time limit on emotions. Adjusting to life without your spouse is painful.

2. Anticipate situations that might be difficult because of memories they will evoke, such as going to a favorite restaurant or doing things you used to enjoy with your spouse. For example, the first time a friend of mine took an airplane flight (her husband had been a pilot) and saw all the pilots, she was overcome with grief. Had she anticipated this first, she may have been better prepared for her reaction.

3. Balance having solace and having people around. This, of course, will depend on your own "wiring."

4. Don't make any major decisions, such as selling your home or making major investments, during the first year. Sometimes those decisions are made to avoid feeling the pain and may be regretted later.

5. Consider keeping a journal to record your thoughts, feelings, and emotions. This will give you a sense of accomplishment and purpose when you see the things you *have* been able to do.

6. Grieve with your children, although you will all grieve differently. Talk about Dad or Mom. Tell family stories. "I remember when Dad would . . . " It's healthy to let your children remember their parent, regardless of their ages. Listen to what they are really telling you by their words, their actions, and their silences. Words give only part of the story.

7. Don't have an expectation of when you will feel better. There is sometimes a misconception that "if I can just get through the first year, everything will be *much* better." Some find that the second year is as difficult because they anticipated

once they had gone through all the "firsts"—first anniversary, first birthday, first Mother's Day or Father's Day, first Christmas—that the next year would be easy. Years later, you may experience "shadow grief" in the weeks just prior to and after the anniversary of a loved one's death. This may include lethargy, depression, and anger similar to the first grief.

8. Avoid chemical aids, such as alcohol, drugs, or sleeping pills, to deaden the pain. If sleeping aids are necessary, be careful about developing a dependency.

9. Seek professional counseling, especially if you feel suicidal. Families, friends, and employers may not understand if they feel you should be over your grief.

10 Keep appropriately busy. Work can be very therapeutic; however, you need time to grieve. Guard against keeping busy to avoid feeling the pain, thus delaying the grieving process.

11. Exercise regularly and maintain healthy eating habits.

12 Ask God for His help and His direction. He has promised to give rest to the weary. Matthew 11:28 says, "Come to me, all you who are weary and burdened, and I will give you rest."

13. Surround yourself with a community of faith, those Christ-followers who can encourage, support, and pray for you.

14. Remember that loneliness and solitude are descriptive of the widowed person's lifestyle. There is a new vulnerability, and recognition of those pieces of the healing journey actually helps in the process.

15. Choose someone who has walked this path before you, and ask for guidance and encouragement.

16. Here are some Scriptures for comfort and guidance:

> The LORD is my shepherd; I shall not be in want.
> He makes me lie down in green pastures,
> he leads me beside quiet waters,
> he restores my soul.
> He guides me in paths of righteousness

    for his name's sake.
Even though I walk
    through the valley of the shadow of death,
I will fear no evil,
    for you are with me;
your rod and your staff,
    they comfort me.
You prepare a table before me
    in the presence of my enemies.
You anoint my head with oil;
    my cup overflows.
Surely goodness and love will follow me
    all the days of my life,
and I will dwell in the house of the LORD
    forever. (Psalm 23:1-6)

I will instruct you and teach you in the way you should go;
I will counsel you and watch over you. (Psalm 32:8)

Now is your time of grief, but I will see you again and you
will rejoice, and no one will take away your joy.
(John 16:22)

For your Maker is your husband—the LORD Almighty is
his name—the Holy One of Israel is your Redeemer; he is
called the God of all the earth. (Isaiah 54:5)

The LORD is close to the brokenhearted and saves those
who are crushed in spirit. (Psalm 34:18)

Sing to God, sing praise to his name, extol him who rides on the clouds—his name is the LORD—and rejoice before him. A father to the fatherless, a defender of widows. (Psalm 68:4-5)

PART 6

Troubled Marriages and Divorce

I cry aloud to the LORD;
I lift up my voice to the LORD for mercy.
I pour out my complaint before him;
before him I tell my trouble.
When my spirit grows faint within me,
it is you who know my way.
In the path where I walk
men have hidden a snare for me.

PSALM 142:1-3

MARRIAGE AND DIVORCE

This section does not contain a theological discussion of divorce. Its purpose is to help pastoral caregivers minister to couples who come seeking help in their pain and to divorced persons who seek compassion and understanding.

As divorce rates have escalated in Christian marriages, it is vital for the church to realize the essential role in caring for these wounded families. Caregivers must avoid taking sides, as it will diminish our effectiveness to minister.

Those who have gone through a divorce often struggle with enormous feelings of failure, guilt, hurt, and rejection. Divorce rips people apart. It is the death of a marriage, which produces feelings similar to those produced by physical death. Even so, the pain of divorce is unique. Pastoral caregivers need to be available to help through the entire process of divorce, offering affirmation and encouragement.

Keep in mind that children are the "silent victims" of divorce. Some sustain more losses than they can handle—perhaps the loss of a parent, a home, financial stability, friends, grandparents, a neighborhood, a school, a church, pets, siblings, and the loss of sense of family. Let them be a part of your world, because it has stability when their world is turning upside down.

Recognize it is not your responsibility to bring healing to broken marriages. Rather, your role is to open lines of communication, to help the couple hear and understand each other, to "translate" misunderstood communication, and to draw out the unspoken.

It is a privilege to be used by God as a listener who may help facilitate communication in a grace-filled, nonjudgmental setting.

COUNSELING COUPLES WHOSE MARRIAGES ARE STRUGGLING

When you are doing pastoral counseling with couples whose marriages are in trouble, keep the following in mind:

1. Set wise, prayerful ground rules in a controlled situation. Be prepared for emotions to surface quickly and vehemently. Expect tears and anger.
2. Keep in mind that rarely is there a villain and a victim. There are normally two sides to the story, and both need to be heard. Listen carefully, lovingly, and impartially, and resist the temptation to take sides or pronounce judgment.
3. Realize a quick resolution is not likely. Couples in trouble have spent months and years building to this crisis. Crisis care can help them have resources and inner controls to communicate on a helpful level, perhaps for the first time in a long time.
4. Remember that you are there to facilitate communication, to help the couple really "hear" each other, often by reflecting back what they say. You are there to help the couple identify and pursue options.
5. Help each party recognize the need for personal responsibility. As long as each person focuses on what the other ought to do, the conflict will continue. When the focus turns to "what I can do to make my marriage work," healing can begin.
6. Find out how both of them perceive God. This is important information for you to know in proceeding with care for the couple.

When You Meet with the Couple
1. Listen. Too often, pastors feel it is their duty to set a couple straight as quickly as possible, so they hand the couple formulaic, insensitive advice without listening. A simple listening technique is to rephrase what you hear the couple telling you.

"Jean, the way you see it is that John has been emotionally distant from you for five years. Is that accurate?" If you cannot rephrase and report back to them what you were just told, you probably didn't hear it.

2. Suggest that the couple speak to each other, rather than about or around each other, or to you.

3. Help the couple determine what the core betrayal is. Many couples assume that love (*eros*, being "in love") sustains their commitment to their partner and must, therefore, be their focus. This misleading assumption builds a perfect stage on which the betrayal dynamics in marriage are acted out.

Keep in mind that most marital struggles — whether emotional, sexual, or spiritual — are about betrayal, and betrayal is about expectations. There is something about dashed expectations — whether or not those expectations are reasonable, formal, or implied — that cuts to the core of our sense of well-being. We want to believe we can count on things, that there is a degree of certainty, safety, and security in our lives. When this security is threatened or violated, the response may be mild or severe, ranging from disappointment, sadness, and depression to outrage, vengeance, emotional sabotage, or even suicide. Marriage is especially susceptible to damage from betrayed expectations. Our response to these betrayals is almost always at the heart of what goes wrong.

Marital betrayals are usually subtle and relatively innocuous at first. His wife knows that he likes to eat dinner at six o'clock, but she somehow manages to drag her briefcase through the door at six forty-five most evenings. Her husband knows how sensitive she is to criticism — especially in public — but can't resist telling their friends about how bad she looks in the mornings. Over time, these "betrayals" increase in volume and intensity until they become "thematic" in nature ("He doesn't have an emotional bone in his body!" "She expects everyone to do everything for her!").

4. Don't be misled by what sometimes appears to be a core betrayal that is simply the most visible manifestation of something even more critical (for example, the affair, which points to the more fundamental betrayal of both emotional and physical fidelity).

5. Help the couple "normalize" (not to be confused with "minimize") the betrayals by saying things like "As difficult and hopeless as this situation may seem to you at times, believe it or not, it is quite common for couples to go through such things." Help them see that neither party is innocent of being the betrayer, and that individual ownership (confession), restitution (atonement), and a significant measure of forgiveness and grace are the means by which restoration occurs. It is not your responsibility to mend the broken relationship.

6. Determine whether the couple is egg- or puzzle-oriented. We are usually taught that marriage is like an egg, the perfect receptacle for love; it is perfect in structure, but also intrinsically fragile. According to this view, it is the job of each spouse to ensure that the egg is neither dropped nor broken. The one who first fails in this assignment—either deliberately or inadvertently—is the principal betrayer. Egg couples usually try to make the case that it was the other who first betrayed the relationship. Egg-energy is all about determining who the primary dropper-of-the-egg is and finding creative ways in which to punish that person. (Most people see marriage this way.)

The other model says marriage is more like a puzzle. We are given stewardship of a box (commitment to marriage). Inside are many pieces of a puzzle. The pieces are all there—a few, in fact, already linked together—but they must be handled, moved, turned over, positioned, and experimented with before the picture begins to emerge.

The distinction between the egg and puzzle models is a significant one: The egg model assumes a defensive posture, while the puzzle model assumes a creative one. Simply put, the egg model is fear driven ("Don't drop the egg!"), while the puzzle model is grace and creativity driven ("Working together, let's see what kind of portrait we can create from these many pieces").

7. According to 2 Peter 1:5-7, the natural progression of spiritual things is from faith to love; that love (*agape*) is the *end* product of *faith*. One can immediately see how this applies to marriage.

   With this passage in mind, suggest that the central challenge of marriage is to determine how each "piece" of their marriage might be handled, and that marriage is a relationship that progresses from faith to love.

8. Help them in any practical way you can. Don't assume that every troubled marriage is the result of some deeply flawed relationship. Sometimes a good job lead can make all the difference. Help the couple tap the resources available to them, which might be anything from becoming involved in a small group or receiving ongoing pastoral support to having personal mentors or professional counseling.

9. Be appropriate and Christ-honoring at all times, fully aware of dependency and attraction that can occur between the hurting person and the caregiver.

10. Speak the truth in love, as the Scripture admonishes us.

This section has been used with permission from M. Wayne Brown, MDiv, LMFT, a private therapist living in Denver, Colorado, and the author of Living the Renewed Life *and* Water from Stone.

HELPFUL INFORMATION FOR DIVORCING OR DIVORCED PARENTS

While children may be better off in a happy one-parent home than in an unhappy two-parent home, the fact remains that divorce is a traumatic event for children. While you are dealing with your own pain, you need to realize the grief that your children are experiencing. The less hostility there is between you and the other parent, the better adjusted your kids will be.

Divorced parents who maintain an affable relationship with each other and who continue to show love and support to their children can lessen the disruptive effects of their separation. It is vital that the parent who does not have custody spend time with the children. If that is not possible, an appropriate prayer for the single parent is that God will bring into the life of the child a "significant other" who will help fill that need. Note that I said "will *help* fill that need"—grief will still surface in a variety of ways.

Society may condition children to trust only their own parents; as a result, they may enter a reconstituted family with feelings of suspicion, overcautiousness, and resentment. Even children's literature, with the wicked stepmother as a recurring character, adds to the problem. Stepparents may try hard to be loving and caring to their stepchildren, but they usually retreat to a less active role when they are rebuffed. Stepparents need to be patient and to resist the temptation of trying to replace the natural parent. They need to realize that they may be competing with an ideal: a person who, in the eyes of the child, is perfect.

Listed below are different reactions your children may be having to your divorce, as well as some things you can do to help them in each stage.

- ❧ *Fear and anxiety.* Divorce will almost always come as a surprise to your children. Give quiet reassurances and discuss plans clearly. Be honest! Love each child openly and frequently. For example, bedtime may be particularly frightening for a young child, so take time for bedtime rituals: read a story, tell a joke, sing a song, pray—even when you are hurting and don't "have the energy."

❧ *Abandonment and rejection.* The divorce has probably brought confusion by dividing the child's loyalties between Mom and Dad. A child will think, *If my dad really loved me, he wouldn't leave me.* Children have difficulty understanding that their parents' separation from each other does not mean that they are separating from their children. As much as possible, be present with the child. Avoid escaping from your own pain by leaving your child with sitters, particularly during the early days of the separation. Talk with your children openly, saying that Mom and Dad both love them.

❧ *Aloneness and very deep sadness.* Things are quieter, and there is more time for children to have fantasies. Take time for tears, and time for fun. Even simple things, such as playing a game or working on a puzzle, can help children see that there can be fun times in spite of sadness.

❧ *Frustration and anger.* Your kids are not getting what they want, which is essentially security, happiness, and a return to the way things were. This can create a deep frustration in them that turns to anger. This anger occasionally turns inward, and they may hurt themselves. Be sensitive to the need for counseling for your children. They may have lived with months or years of conflict in the house.

❧ *Rejection and resentment.* During this stage, children are not over their anger, but they now use emotional distance, the silent treatment, and rejection to punish their parents. Do not try to talk children out of their resentment. Rather, listen respectfully and attempt to draw their feelings out, but also hold to a regularly established routine for bedtime, church activities, and family gatherings. Allow the silent treatment by your teen, if that is where he or she is.

❧ *Taking on the parental role.* Sometimes a child will try to take the absent parent's place, which forces the child into an adult role; yet the child is not prepared to think like an adult, with all the responsibilities that includes. This sense of responsibility, either imposed by the parent or self-imposed, leads to confusion, ambiguity, and frustration.

❧ *Reestablishment of trust.* This stage may take a few months or a few years to arrive at. When it comes, it is like a fresh spring breeze. To facilitate this, a parent may do the following:

- Try not to be preoccupied with your own feelings.
- Allow time for healing.
- Maintain a stable environment.
- Don't become defensive or assign blame.

PART 7

Addiction

I can do everything through him who gives me strength.
PHILIPPIANS 4:13

TYPES OF ADDICTIONS

More than likely, someone in your church is struggling with an addiction, whether it is to alcohol, food, pornography, sex, illegal drugs, prescription drugs, gaming, shopping, or gambling. It is important for pastoral caregivers to realize that many addicts seek help under the guise of a different "presenting problem." Addicts do not see their addiction as destructive because they use alcohol or pornography or some other avenue to numb their feelings. So you may be called to come alongside a troubled family for a different crisis and then discover an underlying addiction in the process of giving care.

Substance and behavioral abuses are attempts to deaden pain: the pain of rejection, loneliness, fear, anxiety, or any of a dozen other hurts. In the long run, instead of making the pain better, the addictive behavior makes the pain worse, as the person experiences deepening humiliation and loss of control.

The rules in an addictive family are *don't trust, don't talk, don't feel*. The addicted person thrives on chaos, which deflects from the real issue. The world revolves around the addict, and that person becomes very myopic in his or her view of life. What are his or her needs? When is the next drink or drug or the next time he or she can get on the Internet? Addiction is a disease that touches every area of an addict's life. When you're an addict, you'll do anything to "protect your supply"; therefore, enabling an addict causes that person to short-circuit the consequences of his or her addiction.

Probably the most important factor in long-term recovery from an addiction is accountability. Lack of accountability allowed the problem to develop, and lack of accountability will lead the addict back into the problem. We as a church, ministering to those who are caught in the trap of addiction, must be willing to walk beside them, listen to them, love them, and confront them.

It can be difficult for those who don't have an addiction to understand just how the addicted person or their loved ones feel. As you walk beside those who are struggling, remember that all of us are in recovery; we're all born with an addiction to sin. Jesus came to set the captives free! We must be Jesus to those who are trapped in *any* form of addiction.

What You Need to Know When Working with the Addicted

Here are some things pastoral caregivers and the families of addicts need to know about addicts and addiction:

Three Things That Contribute to Addiction

1. *A family history of addiction.* For example, alcoholism isn't inherited, but there does seem to be a genetic link. A person is eight times more at risk to become an alcoholic if one or both parents were addicted. According to AddictionsandRecovery .org, approximately 50 percent of the propensity to addiction is genetic.

2. *The existence of a personal crisis.* Often people start abusing alcohol or an alternate substance at the time of crisis, such as retirement, the death of a loved one, and so on.

3. *A strong cultural influence.* In certain locations and within certain cultural groups, there is an increased risk and incidence of addiction. This is true of a video-gaming addiction, which can begin innocently, as can other forms of addiction. In our culture, alcoholism is often tolerated, not treated, as is sexual addiction.

Clues That a Person May Be Struggling with an Addiction

- Abnormal or bizarre behavior, including physical or emotional abusiveness
- Extreme irresponsibility, causing a disruption in the person's lifestyle, sleep patterns, schoolwork, and family life
- Lying, dishonesty
- Cheating, infidelity
- Ongoing financial problems for no apparent reason; money seems to be disappearing; the addicted person has difficulty keeping a job

- ❧ Disintegrating relationships
- ❧ Disrupted or nonexistent communication in the family

Addiction Is Often Accompanied by Sickness
- ❧ Sickness of the spirit: high incidence of incest, violence, lust
- ❧ Sickness of the mind and emotions: manipulation, slipping job performance, paranoia
- ❧ Sickness of the body: high blood pressure, seizures, blackouts, cancer of the esophagus

Myths About Addicts and Addiction
- ❧ "I can't help the addict because he has to ask for help." Even so, you can do guided intervention with the help of someone trained to do intervention work. No one loses in an intervention, which is an orchestrated attempt to get someone to seek professional help for an addiction or some kind of traumatic event or crisis.
- ❧ "You have to let alcoholics quit on their own." If left on their own, nine out of ten won't quit; they will drink themselves to death.
- ❧ "They have a right to use their addiction of choice; it's their own business."
- ❧ "Efforts to help them will only make things worse."

When Working with an Addict, or the Loved Ones of an Addict . . .
1. Recognize that in order to recover, addicts must admit their addiction and want help in stopping. Denial is one of the major obstacles to starting into recovery. Loved ones around the addict can be a big supporting cast. This is the time to use tough love. Statistics show that it often takes seven years after identification of the addiction for a family to try to begin to intervene. People who do not allow consequences support denial. Detach with love by setting strict boundaries. This may involve a period of time in which you do not contact the

addict. You may have to love him or her from afar.

2. Encourage the family to stop enabling, and instead allow the person to suffer consequences. For instance, if an alcoholic is arrested on a DUI charge, do not be too quick to bail him out.

3. Do a lot of reading about the addiction — become educated. Encourage the family to do so as well.

4. Encourage the addict and the family to get counseling. Suggest Alcoholics Anonymous and other support groups.

5. Refuse to loan an addict money.

6. Refuse to talk to a person who is under the influence. There is no point in talking with a chemical.

7. Remember that you are responsible *to*, not responsible *for*.

8. Confrontation should be done carefully, as a process. First, pray: pray for wisdom for your own involvement as the caregiver; pray for the addict to be open; pray for direction.

9. Involve others — a trained intervener, family members, and friends who can help in the intervention.

Keep in Mind These Cautions

1. Never let an alcoholic "detox" at home alone. Alcoholics need medical help to detox, or they could die.

2. There is no known cure; the addicted person is always in recovery.

3. Instant healings are rare. Without doing the work around recovery, people often turn to another addiction.

Behaviors That Aid in Recovery

- ❧ Avoiding old friends who encourage the addiction.
- ❧ Attending Alcoholics Anonymous meetings or other appropriate programs.
- ❧ Not doing too much; keeping life simple.
- ❧ Avoiding mood-altering drugs.
- ❧ Learning to cope with feelings.
- ❧ Talking — telling his or her story, sharing fears and feelings.

❀ Joining a recovery program with the family members.
   (Addiction is a family disease.)

Signs That the Addict Has Relapsed
❀ Exhaustion
❀ Dishonesty
❀ Impatience
❀ Anger
❀ Argumentativeness
❀ Depression
❀ Frustration at everything
❀ Self-pity
❀ Cockiness
❀ Complacency
❀ Expecting too much from others
❀ Use of mood-altering drugs
❀ Wanting too much too soon
❀ Feeling of omnipotence
❀ Lack of follow-through on personal or spiritual disciplines

If you suspect a relapse, confront the person with your suspicions, but don't be condemning. You have the opportunity to extend grace and hope by helping the person realize he or she can "begin again," reminding him or her of the progress made before the "misstep." You then have the opportunity to suggest that the person get back into a recovery program, counseling, and mentoring.

Guidelines If You and the Family Choose Intervention
1. Involve family members, friends, and co-workers who are directly affected by the addiction.
2. Choose a specific date for the intervention, making sure that the addict is unaware of that date.
3. Involve a trained intervener. Call a local treatment center that specializes in the treatment of addiction, and tell them you

think you need an intervention.

4. Hold a practice intervention (under the guidance of the intervener).

5. Involved parties must come up with and adhere to a "bottom line" statement—that point beyond which the person will not go. For example, "I will no longer call your boss and make an excuse for your absence."

6. Be firm and loving.

7. Even if the addicted person refuses to go immediately into treatment, recovery is a process, and the intervention is a valuable part of that process.

8. The caregiver should know what local clinics and hospitals have both day-treatment and in-patient options, along with the names of therapists who specialize in the treatment of addictions.

Used with permission from Jann Glatz, Certified Addictions Counselor III, Nathrup, Colorado.

The Progression and Recovery of the Chemically Dependent

Chemical dependency is a progressive disease, meaning that without help and treatment, the alcoholic or drug addict will move from the crucial phase to the chronic phase.

Crucial Phase

- The chemical substance becomes an obsession.
- There are occasional decisions not to drink or use the drug.
- When one again "uses," there are feelings of guilt.
- As the dependence on the substance becomes greater, there may be memory blackouts.
- The use of the substance increases.
- Excuses to "use" become more frequent.
- There is an increase in tolerance in the amount consumed.
- There may be grandiose and aggressive behavior.
- Efforts to control usage fail repeatedly.
- Excessive blackouts become routine.
- The user may attempt to disassociate with the "using" culture.
- Without intervention, surreptitious substance use continues.
- Family and "nonusing" friends are avoided.
- As the usage becomes chronic, there is an increased dependency on the substance.

Chronic Phase

- The addict exhibits a loss of ordinary willpower.
- Though there may be vague spiritual desires to quit "using," the addiction "wins."
- The addict exhibits tremors and begins "using" earlier and earlier in the day.
- All alibis and excuses are exhausted.
- Lengthy intoxications become more frequent and have a longer duration.

- There is evident moral deterioration.
- Usually there is persistent remorse.
- Thinking becomes impaired.
- There is a loss of other interests and relationships.
- The addiction impacts work and family.
- There is an obsession with the substance.
- Often a paranoia surfaces.
- There is a neglect of personal hygiene and healthy nutrition.

Behaviors During Treatment and Rehabilitation

- A renewed appreciation for relationships
- A renewed desire to again become healthy physically and spiritually, and a renewed interest in personal appearance
- Clearer thinking
- A decrease in rationalization of bad behavior
- A willingness to accept and deal with consequences of poor choices and behavior
- Healthier self-esteem and self-confidence

THE PROGRESSION AND RECOVERY OF THE FAMILY

The following words and phrases characterize what is going on in the family dealing with addiction:

* Arguments
* Depression
* Distrust
* Intolerance
* Unhappiness
* Suspicion
* Threats made and not carried through
* Problems multiplying
* Worry and irritability
* Imaginary illnesses
* Use of prescribed drugs
* Loss of self-respect
* Defensiveness
* Denial
* Family "secrets" (No one talks openly and honestly about the addiction or the way it impacts each individual.)
* Irrational behavior
* Dishonesty and infidelity
* Isolation and escape
* Jealousy

In contrast, these words paint a picture of families who get help for themselves and their loved one:

* Joy
* Eradication of guilt
* Courage
* Return of self-esteem
* Willingness to tell the truth

- ❦ Love
- ❦ Diminishing fears
- ❦ Positive changes in the daily living pattern
- ❦ Peace of mind
- ❦ Developing optimism
- ❦ Willingness to reach out to others in need
- ❦ Cover-up ceases
- ❦ Spiritual examination
- ❦ Release
- ❦ Openness with others
- ❦ Trust, vulnerability
- ❦ Less need to control
- ❦ Peace returns to the home
- ❦ Happiness
- ❦ Acceptance
- ❦ Return of respect toward one another in the family
- ❦ Appreciates spiritual values
- ❦ Return of confidence
- ❦ Hope

DESCRIPTIONS OF EATING DISORDERS

Eating disorders are becoming more and more common. These disorders are potentially life threatening and typically require professional treatment. The following information can help you discern whether an individual you are concerned about might have a serious eating disorder.

The two primary kinds of eating disorders are anorexia nervosa and bulimia nervosa.

Anorexia Nervosa

- Unhealthy obsession over a body weight inappropriate for age and height; weight loss leading to maintenance of body weight 15 percent below that expected; or failure to make expected weight gain during period of growth, leading to body weight 15 percent below that expected.
- Unrealistic, intense fear of gaining weight or becoming fat, even though underweight; distorted body image.
- Disturbance in the way in which one's body weight, size, or shape is experienced. The person claims to "feel fat" even when emaciated or believes that one area of the body is "too fat," even when obviously underweight.
- In females, absence of at least three consecutive menstrual cycles when otherwise expected to occur (called primary or secondary amenorrhea; a woman is considered to have amenorrhea if her periods occur only following the administration of hormones).

Bulimia Nervosa

- Secretive, recurrent episodes of binge eating (rapid consumption of a large amount of food in a short period of time) and then eliminating the food either through vomiting or using laxatives.

- A feeling of lack of control over eating behavior during the eating binges.
- The person regularly engages in self-induced vomiting, the use of laxatives or diuretics, strict dieting or fasting, or vigorous exercise to prevent weight gain.
- A minimum average of two binge eating episodes a week for at least three months.
- Persistent overconcern with body shape and weight; distorted body image.

HELPING THE EATING DISORDERED

If you as a pastoral caregiver suspect someone has an eating disorder . . .

1. Approach the individual directly, privately, and with compassion. Say you are concerned about the person. Listen to how he or she responds to your concern. Be gentle and loving. The biblical principle of "speaking the truth in love" (Ephesians 4:15) applies here.

2. Avoid focusing remarks solely on weight. For example, do not say the person looks "too thin." It will be interpreted as a compliment. As an alternative, say the person looks unhealthy, seems unhappy; that you care, are concerned; and that help is available. For example, you might say, "I'm concerned about you because you seem to be so unhappy lately and don't look healthy. What can I do to help?"

3. When confronting binge-purging, be straightforward about what you suspect. "I've noticed that you leave the table following every meal and head immediately for the bathroom. I'm concerned that you are deliberately making yourself vomit. What can I do to help you?" Making the observation or raising the question may open the door for the person, especially the bulimic, to confide in someone for the first time. You may have the privilege of being the "listener" who is so needed. (Remember, the eating-disordered person feels a lot of guilt.) Those with eating disorders need someone to listen to them, care for them, and encourage them—without judgment.

4. Offer to check into available resources and even to set up an appointment for an evaluation and go along for support.

5. You may have to deal with anger toward you. Remember that a live, angry friend is better than an ill or dead one.

WHAT TO DO IF THE PERSON REFUSES HELP

Those struggling with an eating disorder often refuse help, especially anorexics. They are still in denial, having convinced themselves that their only problem is that they are carrying too much weight, even when emaciated. Bulimics are more likely to be willing to begin treatment, because the binges are so distressing.

Be patient as you pray for wisdom. Do not be overly pushy or discouraged, but bring up your concern again. Identify others in the person's support network. You may need to enlist the aid of other people whom the person admires, respects, and trusts by asking if they will go with you to talk with the eating-disordered person about your concerns. Sometimes people will refuse help because they have deceived themselves into believing that others do not know about the problem, and they do not want others to know. They want to protect their secret.

If the person continues to refuse help (again, this is common with the anorexic), an intervention by a trained intervener may be necessary. Or the person's parents (or another person in authority) may decide that treatment is necessary. It is possible to hospitalize an underage anorexic or bulimic forcibly if there is a threat of suicide or if the person's physical condition is unstable. However, as with any addiction, for treatment to be effective in the long run, the patient must want help.

A Word About Pornography

Pornography has become a huge problem in our culture. Here is some information that pastoral caregivers need to know.

What Typifies Addiction to Pornography?
- ❧ Preoccupation with the behavior or its preparatory activities
- ❧ Need to increase the intensity and frequency with escalation, whether it is pornography through the Internet, videos, books, magazines, or actual sexual contact
- ❧ Giving up or limiting other activities or involvement because of the behavior
- ❧ Distress, anxiety, or irritability if opportunities are denied
- ❧ Deception (covering up behaviors)

How Is Pornography Different from Other Types of Addiction?
- ❧ Easy access
- ❧ Anonymity
- ❧ Privacy (Instead of entering an X-rated theater, users can enter their own study.)
- ❧ Instant availability

Those who are discovered looking at Internet pornography are often conflicted with a mix of remorse and defensiveness, and think, *It's not hurting anyone; it's just entertainment. All my friends do it.* Many Christians, especially men, visit pornographic Internet sites. TechNewsWorld.com reports that 15 to 20 percent of all website hits at work and on university campuses (including Christian institutions) are for pornographic material. The consequences can be serious: damaged reputation, spiritual guilt, expulsion from school, loss of job, and even divorce.

In a recent article from WorldNews Network, research shows that viewers of violent pornography become more aggressive toward females who anger them. In years past, the main option for viewing pornography was in seedy movie theaters. Today it is available in one's own home through the Internet. Pornography promotes immediate sexual gratification, while healthy sexual love teaches that even intense personal pleasures must include sensitivity to others' needs.

A word to pastoral caregivers: Warn the parents in your congregation about the availability of pornography on the Internet, and advise them to monitor their children's use of the computer. If you are giving pastoral care to a youth or adult who has this addiction, you may want to involve a therapist who is trained in dealing with addictions.

Note: For help with issues related to pornography, log on to www .youthspecialties.com. This website has good information for teens and adults.

A WORD ABOUT GAMING ADDICTION

Gaming is a growing addiction, especially among teen males. This addiction is particularly troubling for our society. It impacts the future life of the person involved in a remarkable way, while being insidious in nature. Those addicted to gaming withdraw from relationships and tend to become underachievers at school and at work, which can cost jobs, family, and self-esteem. They "live the game." In other words, the game becomes their reality. Since the games often promote violence, those who are addicted may be transformed from an outgoing, academically gifted student into someone who is reclusive, depressed, aggressive, and manipulative. Some of the same characteristics of an alcoholic are present in those addicted to gaming.

Up to 90 percent of American youth play video games and up to 15 percent (more than five million) may be addicted, according to data cited in the American Medical Association's council report in 2007.

Parents and pastoral caregivers should watch for . . .

- Changes in behavior, from outgoing to reclusive
- Decline in grades
- Several hours spent playing video games daily
- Increase in aggression toward parents and family members
- Decline in personal habits of hygiene
- Increase in depression and thoughts of suicide

Note: One helpful resource is On-Line Gamers Anonymous (www .olganon.org). Or log on to www.youthspecialties.com. Therapists experienced in dealing with other addictions may also be helpful in dealing with addiction to gaming.

A WORD ABOUT CUTTING

Cutting involves using a sharp object to break through the skin, causing injury and pain. It is an outward expression of an inward pain, a way of coping with the pain of strong emotions. Cutters may be dealing with feelings that seem too difficult to bear or with bad situations they think they cannot change.

Cutting does not *necessarily* mean the person is suicidal, although that is a possibility. It is definitely a cry for help, but not necessarily out of a desire to draw attention.

People who cut are often sensitive, aware, and intelligent but have struggles, feel guilty for cutting, and feel self-critical. They may cut themselves on their wrists, arms, legs, or bellies. Some self-injure by burning their skin with lighted matches or the end of a cigarette.

Pastoral caregivers who aren't trained counselors in this area should refer cutters to a therapist specializing in the issues of cutting, grief, loss, and pain. However, the person who cuts still needs love and grace extended to him or her.

Note: For help with issues related to cutting, log on to www.youthspecialties.com.

PART 8

Domestic Violence

Listen to my prayer, O God,
do not ignore my plea;
I would hurry to my place of shelter,
far from the tempest and storm.
PSALM 55:1,8

GENERAL INFORMATION ABOUT DOMESTIC VIOLENCE

Consider these sobering facts about this problem:

- An estimated 1.3 million women and an estimated 835,000 men are victims of physical assault by an intimate partner every day.
- Nearly one in three adult women experience at least one physical assault by a partner during adulthood.
- Approximately half of the men and women who batter abuse their children as well.
- Boys who witness their fathers beating their mothers are twice as likely to abuse their own wives.
- Girls who have witnessed domestic violence are more likely to stay in an abusive relationship as an adult or to become an abuser.
- Risk factors for domestic violence include financial problems, unemployment, divorce or separation (especially during pregnancy), drug or alcohol abuse by the victim or the perpetrator, suicide attempts by the victim or the perpetrator, and mental illness of the victim or the perpetrator.

Family violence is one of the hidden tragedies in our society—and in far more Christian families than most pastoral caregivers recognize. We need to be more educated about this issue so we can be prepared to come alongside these families and individuals to assess, love, and at times confront and intervene.

Domestic violence involves:

- Violent physical or sexual contact between members of a family or household. Physical abuse may include slapping, shaking, shoving, kicking, hitting, biting, choking, the use of a weapon or an object used as a weapon. Sexual abuse involves forcing or coercing a partner to have sex, and hurting a partner.

- Menacing threats.
- Destruction of property as a means to control.

Domestic violence can happen to anyone of any race, religion, or gender. It affects people of all socioeconomic backgrounds and education levels.

Domestic violence has a cycle that is rather typical, but not all battering relationships follow an exact pattern. In the first phase, or *incident phase*, an incident occurs, and the batterer becomes increasingly emotionally and verbally abusive. Emotional abuse is defined as those behaviors not involving physical force that reduce a person's self-worth. It includes blatantly hostile behaviors, such as name-calling, derogatory comments, persistent shaming and ridiculing, and threats of harm. Also included are acts of indifference, such as not responding to a child's distress, ignoring pleas for help, or ignoring a child's needs for comfort, reassurance, and acceptance. While anyone can act in these ways on occasion, the behavior is abusive if it is deliberate and a characteristic pattern.

During the second phase, or *tension phase*, the tension becomes unbearable, and the violence is most severe at this time. The abuse begins, and the victim feels the need to keep the abuser calm. Even if help comes, the victim may side with the batterer and not cooperate with the person there to help.

After the incident, the batterer is often sorry and very loving and kind, and makes promises to change and that it won't happen again. This is the third phase, or *making-up phase*. The victim loves the batterer and desperately wants to believe the abuse will stop. Things appear to be better.

During the next phase, phase four, or *the calm phase*, the batterer acts like the abuse never happened, and promises made during the making-up phase may never be met.

Caregivers in this situation can offer resources, love, hope, and a strong commitment to listen and to care. It is imperative that you not put yourself or others in harm's way. Recognize your limitations and get help.

If you suspect or become aware of domestic violence in a home where there are children present, you are obligated to notify the Department of Social Services or the local police department. While this is the law required of adults who are in positions of responsibility for children, it is everyone's moral obligation.

This information is taken from www.domesticviolence.org, www.nyawc.org (the New York Asian Women's Center), www.ncadv.org (the National Coalition Against Domestic Violence), www.batteredmen.com, and www.ndvh.org (National Domestic Violence Hotline).

Verbal Abuse or Lack of Conflict Management Skills?

The following principles can be helpful to pastoral caregivers who are assessing whether a troubled couple is engaging in verbal abuse or is lacking good conflict-management skills.

- Threats of physical violence and threats of divorce or child custody battles should be considered verbal abuse.
- If there is a history of physical assault, verbal abuse is likely. Couples with poor conflict-management skills, on the other hand, seldom use physical violence, and when they do, they tend to acknowledge responsibility.
- Typically, only one spouse will use verbal abuse; however, both can initiate hostility if the problem is poor conflict management.
- Verbal abuse involves continual invalidation of at least some of the victim's perceptions (even if there is an apology for assault). In contrast, couples with poor conflict-management skills are more likely to eventually acknowledge one another's viewpoints.
- Until they have received counseling or education, or have had time apart from the offender, verbal abuse victims usually are anxious, confused, and lack confidence in their perceptions of abuse. Poor conflict managers, however, tend to present themselves as more assured and certain about their viewpoints of relationship problems.
- Verbal abusers (and sometimes their victims) avoid disclosing specifics about their violent actions. Poor conflict managers tend to be specific, if asked.
- Most verbal abusers have at least occasional difficulty controlling their emotional reactions when discussing responsibility for their behavior. They may rage, whine, cry, or moan. Poor conflict managers generally remain quiet.

CHARACTERISTICS OF A BATTERED WOMAN

A pastoral caregiver who is seeking to help a victim of domestic violence needs to understand that when the woman is the one being battered, she struggles with a very low opinion of her own worth.

- ✤ She believes what she has been told over and over and over again—that she is the problem; it is her fault. If only she would change, then he would change as well.
- ✤ She has been put down so often that she actually believes she is to blame, and it may make her think she is crazy.
- ✤ She has been led to believe that she no longer has any rights to her own body, her own property, or even her own safety.
- ✤ She is in a no-win situation. She constantly feels guilty, but since it is irrational guilt, she has no way to improve.
- ✤ Her emotional struggles lead to many physical symptoms, such as headaches or intestinal issues.
- ✤ The very help she needs, she often does not get because she has withdrawn from family and friends. She does not feel worthy of their involvement and help.
- ✤ She is often resistant to help that may be offered, due to her extreme fear of reprisal. The caregiver must not back off. Keep lending a listening ear, keep praying, keep encouraging, keep offering hope and help, keep urging her to get help and to get away from the batterer.
- ✤ She is often economically dependent on her batterer. As a caregiver, you can brainstorm options with her. Are there people in your church who might help with temporary employment or emergency funds? Is there a local agency from which you can enlist aid?
- ✤ In spite of everything she has been through, she loves him.
- ✤ She does not understand the biblical teachings on submission and allows for the misinterpretation of control as opposed to mutual submission before God.

- ❧ She rarely fights back and has an unhealthy view of loyalty.
- ❧ She is consumed with fear and guilt.

Characteristics of a Batterer

Pastoral caregivers who are seeking to help victims of domestic violence need to recognize the characteristics of a batterer, whether they are coming alongside the victim (to understand his or her pain) or coming alongside the perpetrator (to understand his or her rationalization).

- ❁ Batterers suffer from a very low opinion of themselves.
- ❁ They most likely have witnessed or suffered abuse as a child.
- ❁ They tend to be very emotionally dependent, yet appear to be aggressive and independent.
- ❁ The Christian batterer tends to distort the biblical teaching on submission to mean that dominance and control over the "submitter" are appropriate.
- ❁ Batterers do not take personal responsibility; they tend to blame others, particularly their spouses.
- ❁ They have not learned appropriate internal controls; therefore, their anger escalates and they explode.
- ❁ Once the abuse cycle has escalated into an incident, and the incident begins to wind down, the batterer is typically very sorry.
- ❁ They obsess about losing their partners and are often very jealous.
- ❁ They have never learned to deal with anger in an appropriate manner.
- ❁ They do not trust people.
- ❁ They do not understand unconditional love.
- ❁ They are very controlling, yet they feel their life is out of control.
- ❁ They feel justified in their violent behavior.

HELPFUL INFORMATION FOR DOMESTIC VIOLENCE VICTIMS

The following information is helpful for any adult you suspect is a victim of domestic violence:

1. First and foremost, violence against you is not acceptable. Not even one time!
2. It is not your fault; the blame lies with the abuser.
3. You cannot help a violent partner by yourself. Get help; call 911.
4. Leave before violence occurs again. Get help from a friend your partner does not know.
5. Get a restraining order.
6. Partner abuse may be physical, psychological, sexual, or the destruction of property. All of these are *abuse*.
7. Allowing abuse to continue does not honor God and is not consistent with Scripture. (Ephesians 5:21 calls for *mutual submission*.)

ESCAPE CHECKLIST FOR VICTIMS OF DOMESTIC VIOLENCE

If a person has been a victim of domestic violence once, it is likely he or she will be battered again. Encourage the person to leave or, at the very least, to plan ahead where he or she will go in a dangerous situation. Here is an escape checklist to give him or her:

1. You may be in the greatest danger when you try to leave. There is help for you, but you must ask for it.
2. Call the police to help you leave if you need it.
3. Keep money hidden where you can get it day or night. Have quick access to valuable jewelry.
4. Make two extra sets of keys for your car and home. Put one in a safe place; give the other to a friend.
5. Have extra clothing ready.
6. Go to a safe place—to friends, family, or a shelter.
7. Talk with someone who understands family violence.
8. Have quick access to originals or copies of the following documents:

   - Social Security numbers (your spouse's, yours, and your children's)
   - Birth certificates (yours and your children's)
   - Bank accounts
   - Insurance policies
   - Marriage license
   - Driver's licenses (yours and your spouse's)
   - Papers of mutual ownership
   - Copies of bills
   - Phone numbers for police, shelters, and social services

PART 9

Rape

Evening, morning and noon I cry out in distress,
and he hears my voice.

<small>PSALM</small> 55:17

WHAT YOU NEED TO KNOW ABOUT THE AFTERMATH OF RAPE

Forcible rape is probably the most frequently committed violent crime in America today. Some professionals believe the number of Christians who are victimized by rape could be extremely high because the church perpetuates wrong views, such as "God protects us if we are following Him" or "That's not a problem in our church."

Rape victims often face a sad predicament when it comes to getting help from their churches. They may sense the church would respond inappropriately or not at all. Consequently, victims of sexual assault are often relieved to talk about their experience to a nonjudgmental person who listens empathically, offering them love, support, and care.

The experience of sexual violence changes people's lives. Their daily routines are disrupted; they experience vulnerability, isolation, and helplessness; they are hypervigilant about the possibility of future victimization and, hence, restrict their usual range of activity.

Rape victims go through four phases of trauma:

1. Phase one, the acute phase, is *shock*. The victim feels he or she has lost control. This phase can last from a few hours to one or two weeks. Rape victims typically display two emotional styles of stress: expressed or controlled. The expression might be crying, shaking, smiling, laughing, restlessness, or tenseness. In others, feelings are masked or hidden.
2. Phase two, *outward adjustment*, may last a few months. The victim attempts to get on with life as usual. Symptoms include denial, suppression, rationalization, a decrease in anxiety, and a reluctance to seek help.
3. Phase three, *integration*, begins when the victim develops an inner sense of depression and realizes an urgent need to communicate with those around him or her.
4. Phase four, *resolution*, is the final phase, and has two distinct stages. The first is often triggered by an incident that reminds

the victim of the assault, and a flashback of the event occurs. The symptoms regress to the fears he or she felt in phase one: anxiety, physical complaints, generalized depression, guilt and shame, nightmares, and isolation. The second stage leads to an acceptance of the assault as part of his or her past and allows the person to move on with his or her life.

One of the strongest predictors of ongoing trauma following sexual assault is the presence of one or more important people in the victim's support network who are overtly or covertly unsupportive. These people make such comments as "If you hadn't had on that outfit, it would never have happened," or "What can you expect with the kinds of friends you have?"

HELPING THE VICTIM OF RAPE

Pastoral caregivers have the opportunity to provide a healing environment for survivors of rape and to offer support, guidance, and spiritual hope, particularly as survivors often struggle with guilt and shame. You as the caregiver may be the one "safe place" for the victim to talk, cry, and express feelings of rage and anger toward the assailant.

Here are some things you can do to help:

1. If the rape has just occurred and the victim asks you to come, go immediately. Take or meet her at the nearest hospital emergency room just as she is, without cleaning herself or destroying any evidence, wherever and whenever it occurred: in her car, in her home, or elsewhere.

2. Tell the victim that it is important to give an account of the attack as soon as possible. Reporting it to the police maintains the option to prosecute, should he or she choose to do so.

3. Do not push for specific details if the victim is not ready to share.

4. The victim's feelings are simply feelings; they are not wrong. Strongly encourage him or her to seek professional counseling to help deal with these feelings. Your role is to offer support, not therapy. Support involves walking alongside; therapy involves treatment.

5. Reflect back to the person the feelings that are expressed to you. He or she may say, "How could I have been so stupid?" Your response may be something like "How could you possibly have been prepared for something like this?"

6. As in all pastoral counseling, the information about a rape must remain confidential.

7. Help the victim process the many decisions, details, and questions he or she will face when relating to police, family, friends, advocates, and hospital personnel.

8. Encourage the victim to get help. His first inclination may

be to hide his shame and ignore what he has been through. Encourage him that rape crisis centers can be extremely helpful. They understand the trauma a victim is going through.

9. Remind her that she is *not* the criminal; she is the victim.

10. While it is his or her decision whether or not to report the rape and file charges against the attacker, encourage the victim to seek godly, wise counsel in making those decisions.

11. Secret keeping causes problems later on and will make victims feel powerless. Encourage them to share with loved ones, and tell them that you will be privileged to be with them every step of the way.

12. Pray for wisdom and that God will speak through you, reminding them how much He loves them. However, be careful to go at their pace. Be careful not to impose biblical truths that they are not yet ready to hear.

13. Encourage them to resume their lifestyle as much as possible. They may not feel safe if the attack happened at home. Discuss these fears as soon as they are able.

14. Remind the victim that grief is a process and will take time and that you will walk through the process with him or her.

WHEN THE MEMORY JUST OCCURRED

If you are offering pastoral care to someone who suddenly remembers a rape that happened in the past . . .

1. Listen *before* speaking.
2. Encourage the man or woman to share the complete story, and be willing to listen, though the story may be difficult to hear.
3. Speak truth into his or her life. Most often rape victims have believed lies about themselves. They may believe they caused the rape; that they are unworthy of healthy intimate relationships; that there is no hope for healing; that they need to just bury the memory again and maintain an unhealthy lifestyle as they have known it since the rape occurred. Remind them that Jesus said, "The truth will set you free" (John 8:32).
4. Encourage professional counseling. Often an undealt-with rape or sexual assault will lead to a life of promiscuity or an inability to be intimate. Just knowing that fact will be helpful to the person who struggles with guilt. Telling his or her story is the first step toward healing. Now he or she needs counseling to deal with these past, hidden issues. Be prepared with counseling referrals.
5. Offer to pray with and for him or her for God's truth and His hope and healing.
6. If it feels right, share these Scriptures:

> To the LORD I cry aloud, and he answers me from his holy hill. I lie down and sleep; I wake again, because the LORD sustains me. (Psalm 3:4-5)

> Answer me when I call to you, O my righteous God. Give me relief from my distress; be merciful to me and hear my prayer. . . . Let the light of your face shine upon us, O LORD. (Psalm 4:1,6)

O LORD, hear my prayer,
    listen to my cry for mercy;
in your faithfulness and righteousness
    come to my relief.
Do not bring your servant into judgment,
    for no one living is righteous before you.
The enemy pursues me,
    he crushes me to the ground;
he makes me dwell in darkness
    like those long dead.
So my spirit grows faint within me;
    my heart within me is dismayed.
I remember the days of long ago;
    I meditate on all your works
    and consider what your hands have done.
I spread out my hands to you;
    my soul thirsts for you like a parched land.
Answer me quickly, O LORD;
    my spirit fails.
Do not hide your face from me
    or I will be like those who go down to the pit.
Let the morning bring me word of your unfailing love,
    for I have put my trust in you.
Show me the way I should go,
    for to you I lift up my soul.
Rescue me from my enemies, O LORD,
    for I hide myself in you.
Teach me to do your will,
    for you are my God;
may your good Spirit
    lead me on level ground.
For your name's sake, O LORD, preserve my life;
    in your righteousness, bring me out of trouble.
In your unfailing love, silence my enemies;
    destroy all my foes,
    for I am your servant. (Psalm 143:1-12)

HELPFUL INFORMATION FOR PARENTS OF A RAPE VICTIM

If your son or daughter tells you he or she was raped . . .

1. Believe him or her. Your child has gone through a traumatic experience and needs your support, courage, and love. He or she does not need judgment or blame from you. Your child is the victim of a crime. It took a great deal of courage to tell you.
2. If the rape just occurred, get help immediately. He or she needs to be taken to the nearest hospital emergency room. If the incident happened in the past, be sensitive to the potential need for counseling.
3. Assure your child of your support over and over again. Listen without judgment.
4. Do not try to cover up what has happened, ignore it, or push him or her to get over it. Healing from traumatic grief is a long, difficult process.
5. Recognize that sometimes girls or boys don't tell their parents about a rape because they are afraid of what their dad might do to them (be angry, ground them, call them names) or to the perpetrator (this is particularly true if the parents know the rapist). You as the parents need to deal with your own anger without complicating your child's grief process with uncontrolled rage toward the assailant.

HELPFUL INFORMATION FOR THE SPOUSE OF A RAPE VICTIM

If a married woman in your congregation is raped, share the following with her husband:

1. Believe her. She needs your support. Your wife is the victim of a violent crime.
2. Recognize how difficult it was for her to tell you. She is and will be experiencing many fears — that you will reject her; that you will not believe her; that you will think she could have done something to prevent the rape; that you will not love her anymore.
3. Love her. Listen to her. Do not judge her. Care for her in the unique ways you know your wife needs. Do not push for more details than she is ready to tell you. At the same time, be willing to listen when she needs to talk with you.
4. Be patient with her, particularly in setting the pace in resuming sexual intimacy. Remember, she has been traumatized beyond what you can imagine. She needs to know that you trust her so that she can trust you. Be very sensitive to her needs.
5. Counseling will be helpful for both of you. Assure her that you are willing to go with her for either individual or couples counseling. This is not just her problem to work through; you have been traumatized as well.

PART 10

Forgiveness

If we confess our sins, he is faithful and just and will forgive us our sins and purify us from all unrighteousness.
1 John 1:9

FORGIVENESS

"If we confess our sins, he is faithful and just and will forgive us our sins and purify us from all unrighteousness" (1 John 1:9). Jesus forgives us; however, we often are not as quick to forgive ourselves or others. Wrapped up in the whole topic of forgiveness is our ongoing struggle with shame, guilt, and God's grace.

This section briefly touches on the challenges of dealing with forgiveness, the lies that so often surround the subject of forgiveness, the benefits of forgiveness, and some of the how-tos.

When he was reunited with his estranged brother Esau, Jacob declared, "For to see your face is like seeing the face of God, now that you have received me favorably" (Genesis 33:10). That is a description of forgiveness.

In our care for others, let us share God's grace.

WHAT PEOPLE NEED TO KNOW ABOUT FORGIVENESS

If you are counseling people who need to forgive, here are some things they may need to know about what forgiveness is, what it is not, and how to forgive.

What Forgiveness Is

The Greek verb for forgiveness (*aphiemi*) means "to send away, to give up, to let go."

According to Webster, *forgiveness* means "to cease to feel resentment against an offender; to give up resentment of or claim to requital for an insult or injury; to grant relief from a payment due on a debt." Consider that definition again:

- To cease to feel resentment . . .
- Against an offender . . .
- To give up resentment or claim . . .
- For an injury . . .
- To grant relief . . .
- From a payment due on a debt

In other words, *forgiveness* means "to choose to willingly give up one's legitimate rights for repayment — and one's tools of punishment — both now and in the future."

Reasons to Forgive

- ❀ Jesus commanded it (see Matthew 6:12,14).
- ❀ Not forgiving hinders our relationship with God (see Matthew 6:15).
- ❀ When we forgive, we can better understand and respond to God's grace in our own lives (see Colossians 3:12-13).
- ❀ Forgiveness frees us for the future and for restored relationships (see Genesis 45:4-15).

What Forgiveness Does Not Do

- ❧ Forgiveness does not equal forgetting. (Has Jesus forgotten the cross? No, but He has forgiven the pain caused.)
- ❧ Forgiveness does not address the issues that caused the injury. There may still need to be consequences for sins committed.
- ❧ Forgiveness does not release anyone from being responsible for a wrong done.
- ❧ Forgiveness is not a one-time event. Jesus says in 1 John 1:9 that we need to confess our sins. When we sin, we need to confess; when we sin again, we need to confess. Both confession and forgiveness are ongoing.

Lies People Believe About Forgiveness That Keep Them from Forgiving

- ❧ "If I can get even, then I'll feel better. Maybe then I'll forgive."

    But the truth is . . . vengeance is a damaging problem, not a solution.

- ❧ "When I blame those who have hurt me, I don't hurt as much. Forgiving will cause *me* to feel all the pain."

    But the truth is . . . blaming transfers nothing; it only chains you to the pain.

- ❧ "I'll just ignore the hurt and bitterness, and eventually it will go away. When it doesn't hurt anymore, it'll be easier to forgive."

    But the truth is . . . ignore a wound, and it festers and grows worse.

- ❧ "I don't have to forgive. I can make it all up to everyone involved and balance the score some other way."

    But the truth is . . . God commands us to forgive even as He forgave us.

- ❧ "People need to be on *my* side. With their support, I feel better. If I truly forgive, others might not rally to support me as much."

> *But the truth is . . . do you really want people to support you out of pity?*

❧ "Sure, I'll forgive—in about ten years. You've gotta give me time."

> *But the truth is . . . unforgiveness drains your energy more and more each day.*

❧ "If I forgive, people may see me as weak and take advantage of me."

> *But the truth is . . . God forgives all the time. Is He weak?*

❧ "It's too embarrassing to seek forgiveness after all that happened."

> *But the truth is . . . we can be embarrassed for a moment or remain trapped.*

❧ "They need to admit they were wrong. I'll forgive when and if those who hurt me ask for forgiveness."

> *But the truth is . . . forgiveness is for us, not them. We must choose.*

❧ "The pain is a part of who I am. It's been with me so long."

> *But the truth is . . . you can stay stuck forever, or you can let God touch your pain.*

Why Forgive

❧ To be free of the past
❧ To be free of the pain
❧ To break the cycle of retribution
❧ To minimize unintentionally hurting or offending others
❧ To begin the process of healing and growth
❧ To gain (regain) a sense of personal dignity
❧ To understand and demonstrate an actual, rubber-on-the-road type of Christianity
❧ Because God commands it: "For if you forgive men when they sin against you, your heavenly Father will also forgive you. But if you do not forgive men their sins, your Father will not forgive your sins" (Matthew 6:14-15).

Remember, in almost all cases, the *forgiver* receives the benefit.

Keys to Forgiveness
1. Choose to give up your perceived right to get even (see 1 Peter 3:9).
2. Choose not to hold the offense over someone's head (see Romans 12:18).
3. Try to put the past in the past and move ahead in the relationship as Joseph did (see Genesis 50:20).
4. Recognize that your offenders are responsible for their behavior and you are responsible for yours (see John 8:3-11).
5. Recognize that forgiveness is often a process, not an event.

Whom to Forgive
1. Yourself—place to start
2. The person who hurt, betrayed, or offended you
3. The other involved parties
4. God (He doesn't need it—He's sinless—but it does free us up)

How to Forgive
1. *Be honest with yourself and with others*. If you have been offensive or offended someone, do not be defensive, but go to the other person and make it right (see Matthew 5:23-24; Mark 11:25).

   > You are truly my disciples if you live as I tell you to, and you will know the truth, and the truth will set you free. (John 8:31-32, TLB)

2. *Seek wisdom and understanding*. Ask God for wisdom (see James 1:5), helping you to clarify the issues requiring forgiveness.

Getting wisdom is the most important thing you can do! And with your wisdom, develop common sense and good judgment. (Proverbs 4:7, TLB)

3. *Forgive as many times as needed* to convince yourself that you've completely forgiven the other person.

I tell you, not seven times, but seventy-seven times. (Matthew 18:22)

4. *Make recompense if needed and if possible.* Honor your own responsibilities by asking for forgiveness when you have been the offender. As Psalm 139:23-24 reminds us, God is the One who will reveal to us our faults.

Do not gloat when your enemy falls; when he stumbles, do not let your heart rejoice, or the LORD will see and disapprove. (Proverbs 24:17-18)

5. *Let go. Let go. Let go.*

The LORD will fight for you; you need only to be still. (Exodus 14:14)

6. *Be open to the reconciliation process.* That process includes personal examination of your own part in the need for reconciliation.

Why do you look at the speck of sawdust in your brother's eye and pay no attention to the plank in your own eye? (Matthew 7:3)

Let the peace of Christ rule in your hearts, since as members of one body you were called to peace. And be thankful. (Colossians 3:15)

Resources

RESOURCES

This section includes a number of books that I have found helpful in my work as a pastoral caregiver. They are organized alphabetically by these topics:

- ✢ Abortion
- ✢ Abuse
- ✢ Addiction
- ✢ Adult Children of Alcoholics
- ✢ Aging Parents
- ✢ AIDS and HIV
- ✢ Cancer/Illness/Pain
- ✢ Christianity
- ✢ Codependency
- ✢ Crisis Intervention
- ✢ Death/Grief
- ✢ Death/Grief and Children
- ✢ Depression
- ✢ Divorce
- ✢ Domestic Violence
- ✢ Dysfunctionalism
- ✢ Emotions
- ✢ Encouragement
- ✢ Family
- ✢ Forgiveness
- ✢ Grief
- ✢ Homosexuality
- ✢ Listening
- ✢ Marriage
- ✢ Menopause
- ✢ Miscarriage
- ✢ Parenting
- ✢ Physical Loss/Chronic Pain

🍂 Rape
🍂 Sexual Addiction/Pornography

ABORTION

Cochrane, Linda, and Kathy Jones. *Healing a Father's Heart: A Post-Abortion Bible Study for Men*. Grand Rapids, MI: Baker, 1996.
> Babies' fathers grieve too, but often their grief is expressed very differently from that of mothers. This book puts words to the grief of fathers—expressing the emotions that they are feeling—and gives hope for healing.

Freed, Luci, and Penny Yvonne Salazar. *A Season to Heal: Help and Hope for Those Working Through Post-Abortion Stress*. Nashville: Thomas Nelson, 1993.
> Freed and Salazar give God-honoring insight to those who struggle with the grief of abortion, helping them to move through their personal journeys of guilt and sadness to a place of healing.

ABUSE

Allender, Dan B. *The Wounded Heart: Hope for Adult Victims of Childhood Sexual Abuse*. Rev. ed. Colorado Springs, CO: NavPress, 2008.
> An intensely personal and specific look at sexual abuse, this book goes well beyond the general issues and solutions discussed in other books. It serves as a good curriculum for support groups for both men and women who have suffered through the trauma of sexual abuse; there is also a companion workbook. Chapter titles include "The Reality of a War," "Deflection," "The War Zone," "Powerlessness," "Betrayal," "Ambivalence," "Secondary Symptoms," "Style of Relating," "The Unlikely Route to Joy," "Honesty," "Repentance," and "Bold Love."

Alsdurf, James, and Phyllis Alsdurf. *Battered into Submission: The Tragedy of Wife Abuse in the Christian Home*. Downers Grove, IL: InterVarsity Press, 1989.

> We in the church have difficulty believing such abuse occurs in Christian homes. This book offers help and a realistic look at this hidden sin. Chapter titles include "A Nightmare in the Christian Home"; "Who Is the Battered Woman and Why Does She Stay?"; "What Kind of Men Abuse Their Wives?"; "Blaming the Victim"; "Wife Abuse and the Submission of Women"; "The Process of Reconciliation"; "Marriage, Divorce and Wife Abuse"; "The Church and Reconciliation"; and "Violence in the Land."

Frank, Jan. *Door of Hope: Recognizing and Resolving the Pains of Your Past*. Rev. ed. Nashville: Thomas Nelson, 1995.

> Jan Frank offers a personal look at abuse with the hope-filled view of healing from such past abuse. Chapter titles include "Healing Emotional Wounds," "Face the Problem," "Recount the Incident," "Experience the Feelings," "Establish Responsibility," "Trace Behavioral Difficulties and Symptoms," "Observe Others and Educate Yourself," "Confront the Aggressor," "Acknowledge Forgiveness," "Rebuild Self-Image and Relationships," and "Restoration—His Redeeming Work."

Heggen, Carolyn Holderread. *Sexual Abuse in Christian Homes and Churches*. Scottdale, PA: Herald Press, 1993.

> This book brings help and hope for anyone caught in or concerned about the abuse cycle. It addresses the brokenness of the victim and the perpetrator.

ADDICTION

B., Bill. *Compulsive Overeater*. Center City, MN: Hazelden Press, 1988.

This book offers help for the person who struggles with an addiction to food. It incorporates the twelve-step program in helping the addicted person on the road to healing and wholeness.

Spickard Jr., Anderson, and Barbara R. Thompson. *Dying for a Drink: What You and Your Family Should Know About Alcoholism*. Waco, TX: Word, 1985.
> This is a great book to recommend to individuals and families struggling with issues relating to alcoholism. The authors give a Christian perspective and a balanced approach to treatment.

ADULT CHILDREN OF ALCOHOLICS

Black, Claudia. *It Will Never Happen to Me: Growing Up with Addiction as Youngsters — Adolescents — Adults*. Center City, MN: Hazelden Press, 2002.
> The author shares an overall perspective — what it is like growing up in an alcoholic home and what recovery might look like. Chapter titles include "Roles"; "Don't Talk, Don't Trust, Don't Feel"; "The Progression of the Roles"; "The Child Within the Home"; and "The Adult Child."

LeSourd, Nancy. *No Longer the Hero: The Personal Pilgrimage of an Adult Child*. Nashville: Thomas Nelson, 1992.
> Nancy LeSourd helps readers to understand the addicted family and to recognize what is not "normal."

AGING PARENTS

Bloomfield, Harold H., and Leonard Felder. *Making Peace with Your Parents*. New York: Random House, 1996.
> The title describes the book — both the issues and the solutions when dealing with aging parents. Find help for communicating true emotions in a loving, respectful way.

Deane, Barbara. *Caring for Your Aging Parents: When Love Is Not Enough.* Colorado Springs, CO: NavPress, 1989.
> Many complicated issues are involved when loving and caring for parents who are aging—setting boundaries, getting help for the caregivers, dealing with issues surrounding health and dying. This book addresses all of these and more.

Seuss, Dr. *You're Only Old Once!* New York: Random House, 1986.
> Are you a Dr. Seuss fan? Then this book, which looks at old age, is for you!

Silverstone, Barbara, and Helen Kandel Hyman. *You and Your Aging Parent: A Family Guide to Emotional, Social, Health, and Financial Problems.* 4th ed. New York: Oxford University Press, 2008.
> The unique benefit of this book on dealing with aging parents is the concept of developing a family "team."

Tournier, Paul. *Learn to Grow Old.* London: Westminster/John Knox, 1991.
> Dr. Tournier leads us to theological, biblical insights about aging and our need to prepare for growing old.

AIDS AND HIV

Christensen, Michael J. *The Samaritan's Imperative: Compassionate Ministry to People Living with AIDS.* Nashville: Abingdon, 1991.
> Looking for a Christ-centered approach as you minister to those with AIDS? Written with sensitivity and compassion by a minister who cares for people living with AIDS every day, this book sweeps away statistics and places readers in the midst of the human reality of AIDS. It looks at people—not disease!

Kübler-Ross, Elisabeth. *AIDS: The Ultimate Challenge.* New York: Simon & Schuster, 1997.

Dr. Kübler-Ross weaves her compassionate heart and her expertise in the field of death and dying into a look at AIDS—giving comfort and helping patients through the critical stages of dying as they face the end of their lives.

CANCER/ILLNESS/PAIN

Anderson, Greg. *The Cancer Conqueror: An Incredible Journey to Wellness*. Dallas: Word, 1988.

This unique book gives us an understanding of a holistic approach to illness—particularly, the disease of cancer. Chapter titles include "The Search for Solutions," "The Perspective of Personal Responsibility," "The Cancer Conqueror Believes," "The Cancer Conqueror Resolves," "The Cancer Conqueror Lives," "The Cancer Conqueror Explains," and "The Cancer Conqueror Benefits."

Brand, Paul, and Philip Yancey. *Pain: The Gift Nobody Wants*. New York: HarperCollins, 1993.

Dr. Brand points out that pain is a necessary part of our lives. In fact, he shows us that it is our ally. He uses the example of those suffering from leprosy—who can feel no pain and are at risk of personal injury because they lack that sensation of pain.

Kreeft, Peter. *Making Sense Out of Suffering*. Ann Arbor, MI: Servant, 1986.

This is a book for the person who is seeking answers to the questions that arise out of suffering.

Yancey, Philip. *Where Is God When It Hurts?* Grand Rapids, MI: Zondervan, 2002.

This classic is revealing, loving, and powerful as it deals realistically with crises of pain and suffering. Yancey guides the reader beyond the pain to the God who never leaves the sufferer. Section titles include "Why Is There Such a Thing as Pain?" "How People Respond to Suffering," and "How Can We Cope with Pain?"

CHRISTIANITY

Hybels, Bill. *Just Walk Across the Room: Simple Steps Pointing People to Faith*. Grand Rapids, MI: Zondervan, 2006.

> Through this practical, hands-on book, Hybels helps all of us understand the value of developing relationships with people who need a Savior. It is not that hard to just love people, get to know them, and tell them what you know about your own faith — that is what we are called to do. This book is an important tool in your personal discipleship.

Little, Paul. *Know Why You Believe*. Downers Grove, IL: InterVarsity Press, 2000.

> This book will help answer tough questions concerning science and Scripture, miracles, and the Christian experience. It is written for seekers of the Christian faith and those wanting to be better equipped to help seekers. Chapter titles include "Is Christianity Rational?" "Is There a God?" "Is Christ God?" "Is the Bible God's Word?" "Does Archaeology Verify Scripture?" "Are Miracles Possible?" "Do Science and Scripture Agree?" "Why Does God Allow Suffering and Evil?" "Does Christianity Differ from Other World Religions?" and "Is Christian Experience Valid?"

CODEPENDENCY

Beattie, Melody. *Beyond Codependency: And Getting Better All the Time*. Center City, MN: Hazelden Press, 1989.

> This book helps the codependent person move toward health. It underscores the need for positive affirmation to counter negative messages.

Beattie, Melody. *Codependent No More: How to Stop Controlling Others and Start Caring for Yourself*. Center City, MN: Hazelden Press, 1992.

> Beattie helps with alternatives and boundaries—both for the person who is struggling with codependency and for the caregiver.

Hemfelt, Robert, Frank Minirth, and Paul Meier. *Love Is a Choice: The Definitive Book on Letting Go of Unhealthy Relationships*. Nashville: Thomas Nelson, 2003.

> The unique aspect of this book on recovery from codependency centers on God's unconditional love. Section titles include "What Codependency Is," "The Causes of Codependency," "Factors That Perpetuate Codependency," "Codependency in Interpersonal Relationships," and "The Ten Stages of Recovery."

CRISIS INTERVENTION

Berkley, James D. *Called into Crisis: The Nine Greatest Challenges of Pastoral Care*. Carol Stream, IL: Christianity Today, 1988.

> This book is a helpful composite of crisis care—looking at subjects such as handling a crisis, marital conflict and divorce, sexual misconduct, domestic violence and abuse, homosexuality, major illnesses and injuries, death of a child, death of a spouse, suicide, and alcohol and drug problems.

Kennedy, Eugene. *Crisis Counseling: The Essential Guide for Nonprofessional Counselors*. New York: Continuum, 1981.

> Guiding readers through a series of commonsense essays, this book gives guidelines for lay counselors, helping them to be more effective in their responses with patients, students, and parishioners.

DEATH/GRIEF

Heatherley, Joyce Landorf. *Mourning Song*. 2nd ed. Grand Rapids, MI: Revell, 1994.

> This book is a look at one woman's grief journey as she shares personal faith stories along with theological reflections.

Komp, Diane M. *A Window to Heaven: When Children See Life in Death*. Grand Rapids, MI: Zondervan, 1992.

> This book is a helpful tool that encourages us to hang on to our faith through our deep life valleys.

Kuenning, Delores. *Helping People Through Grief*. Grand Rapids, MI: Bethany House, 1987.

> Delores Kuenning looks at many aspects of grief through practical how-tos. Topics include terminal illness, SIDS, child abduction and murder, missing or kidnapped children, the birth of handicapped children, and Alzheimer's.

Means, James. *A Tearful Celebration: Finding God in the Midst of Loss*. Sisters, OR: Multnomah, 2006.

> Rev. Means wrote this book after the death of his wife. He explores the death journey, the pain, God's presence, and what's next for the journeyer.

Sproul, R. C. *Surprised by Suffering*. Carol Stream, IL: Tyndale, 1994.

> A noted theologian helps answer tough questions on issues that include our hope for a future life, the fate of suicides and the stillborn, images of heaven, terminal illness, and euthanasia.

Tada, Joni Eareckson. *The Life and Death Dilemma: Families Facing Health Care Choices*. Grand Rapids, MI: Zondervan, 1995.

> As a caregiver, as a family member, or as an individual, we may face life and death decisions. This book addresses many of those questions: "When is it okay to discontinue life

support?" "How much is too much chemotherapy?" "Where is God in all of this?" and "What is His will?"

Westberg, Granger E. *Good Grief: A Faith-Based Guide to Understanding and Healing*. Minneapolis: Augsburg Fortress, 2004.
> This classic grief book gives solid, helpful information and takes the reader through the process of grieving.

DEATH/GRIEF AND CHILDREN

O'Toole, Donna. *Aarvy Aardvark Finds Hope*. Burnsville, NC: Compassion Books, 1988.
> Aarvy has lost his mother and brother to the zoo and is now left alone. His little friend Ralphy Rabbit helps him work through his grief and find hope.

Sanford, Doris, *It Must Hurt a Lot: A Child's Book About Death*. Portland, OR: Multnomah, 1985.
> This children's book addresses loss and death using the example of a boy and his dog. There is help for adults in helping children.

Wolfelt, Alan. *Helping Children Cope with Grief*. Muncie, IN: Accelerated Development, 1983.
> Alan Wolfelt is an expert on grief care, particularly when it comes to grieving children. "If a child is old enough to love, he/she is old enough to grieve." Learn how to help that child. Chapter titles include "When Should Death Education Occur?" "Creating a Caring Relationship: An Open Atmosphere," "Children's Understanding and Response to Death (With Caregiver Behaviors)," "Caregiving Aspects of Helping the Grieving Child (Skills Needed by the 'Helping-Healing-Adult')," and "Preparing to Help Others Help Children."

DEPRESSION

Hart, Archibald D. *Dark Clouds, Silver Linings.* Colorado Springs, CO: Focus on the Family, 1994.

> Dr. Hart helps both the person going through depression and the caregiver better understand depression. He also introduces the biblical aspect of hope. He discusses the nature and causes of depression, coping with depression and overcoming its negative effects, knowing when it's time to seek professional help, and turning depression into a healing emotion.

Welch, Edward T. *Depression: A Stubborn Darkness.* Winston-Salem, NC: Punch Press, 2004.

> Dr. Welch touches upon the spiritual, medical, and emotional aspects of depression. He addresses the complexities that are involved for the struggler and the caregiver and points the reader toward hope.

DIVORCE

Duty, Guy. *Divorce and Remarriage: A Christian View.* Minneapolis: Bethany Fellowship, 1967.

> This classic book gives the biblical approach to divorce and remarriage. Chapter titles include "Christ's Divorce Law in Matthew 5:32," "The Jewish Writing of Divorcement," "The Meaning of Fornication," "Christ's Divorce Law in Matthew 19:9," "Are Fornication Exceptions Genuine?" "The Meaning of Romans 7:1-4," "The Meaning of 1 Corinthians 7:10-15," "The Church Fathers' Views on Divorce and Remarriage," and "Replies to Objections."

Hart, Archibald D. *Healing Adult Children of Divorce: Taking Care of Unfinished Business So You Can Be Whole Again.* Ann Arbor, MI: Vine, 1991.

This is one of the few books written for adult children of divorce. Dr. Hart helps the reader understand what true healing might look like. Topics include how to resolve mistrust and guilt, how to replace blame with forgiveness, how to change your attitude toward yourself, and how to break the divorce cycle in your life.

DOMESTIC VIOLENCE

Fortune, Marie. *Sexual Violence: The Sin Revisited*. Cleveland, OH: Pilgrim Press, 2005.

Marie Fortune is the executive director of the Center for the Prevention of Sexual and Domestic Violence. In this book she breaks the silence of this traumatic hidden sin and addresses it with compassion and depth.

Miles, Al. *Domestic Violence: What Every Pastor Needs to Know*. Minneapolis: Augsburg Fortress, 2000.

What does a pastor do when he is meeting with a person who suddenly discloses that he or she is a victim—or a perpetrator—of domestic violence? Most pastors are not equipped to handle this complex issue. This book includes biblical principles and practical insights.

DYSFUNCTIONALISM

Anderson, Neil T. *The Bondage Breaker: Overcoming Negative Thoughts, Irrational Feelings, Habitual Sins*. Eugene, OR: Harvest House, 2006.

This is a book to give freedom—freedom from hidden sins and the bondage that accompanies those sins. It offers practical, step-by-step help. Chapter titles include "You Don't Have to Live in the Shadows," "Confronting the Rebel Prince," "Jesus Has You Covered," "Dealing with Evil in Person," "The Lure of Knowledge and Power," "Enticed to

Do It Your Way," "Don't Believe Everything You Hear,"
"Appearances Can Be Deceiving," "The Danger of Losing
Control," and "Steps to Freedom in Christ."

Anderson, Neil. *Released from Bondage*. Nashville: Thomas Nelson,
1992.

> Sometimes it helps to hear how others have overcome
> incredible bondage. Read the stories of some who have
> been set free. Chapter titles include "Molly: Freedom from
> the Cycle of Abuse," "Anne: Freedom Through Stages
> of Growth," "Sandy: Freedom from Cultic and Occultic
> Bondage," "Jennifer: Freedom from Eating Disorders,"
> "Nancy: Female Sexual Abuse and Freedom," "Doug: Male
> Sexual Abuse and Freedom," "The Church: Helping People
> to Freedom," and "Freedom from Satanic Ritual Abuse and
> MPD."

EMOTIONS

Hart, Archibald D. *Unlocking the Mystery of Your Emotions*. Dallas:
Word, 1989.

> This book is a good resource when helping people deal with
> their own emotions and those of others. Dr. Hart addresses
> such emotions as anger, guilt, self-hate, and depression and
> helps the reader to understand the gift of our emotions.
> Chapter titles include "What Have You Done with Your
> Emotions?" "Our Confusing Emotions," "How Thoughts
> Cause Emotions," "The Problem of Anger," "Freedom from
> Depression," "Freedom from Self-Hate," "Freedom from
> Guilt," and "Freedom to Be Real."

Seamands, David A. *Healing for Damaged Emotions*. Colorado
Springs, CO: David C. Cook, 1991.

> This is an excellent book on understanding and dealing
> with one's emotions. The chapter on "Healing Our Low

Self-Esteem" is particularly helpful. Other chapter titles include "Damaged Emotions"; "Guilt, Grace, and Debt-Collecting"; "The Wounded Healer"; "Satan's Deadliest Weapon"; "Symptoms of Perfectionism"; "Super You or Real You?"; "Myths and Truths About Depression"; and "Healed Helpers."

Smedes, Lewis B., *Forgive and Forget: Healing the Hurts We Don't Deserve*. New York: HarperCollins, 2007.
    Dr. Smedes encourages us to move beyond bitterness to healing. Section titles include "The Four Stages of Forgiving," "Forgiving People Who Are Hard to Forgive," "How People Forgive," and "Why Forgive?"

ENCOURAGEMENT

Brown, M. Wayne. *Water from Stone: When "Right Christian Living" Has Left You Spiritually Dry.* Colorado Springs, CO: NavPress, 2004.
    Wayne Brown is an author unwilling to live in or with the spiritual status quo. He challenges us to look at all God allows in our lives—from joys to sorrows—as part of His plan.

Johnson, Barbara. *So, Stick a Geranium in Your Hat and Be Happy!* Dallas: Word, 1990.
    Barbara Johnson has experienced pain—a *lot* of pain. She deals with that pain with godly humor and helps the reader through such chapters as "Pain Is Inevitable, but Misery Is Optional"; "I Can Handle Any Crisis—I'm a Mother"; "It's Always Darkest Just Before It Goes Totally Black"; "I Feel So Much Better Now That I've Given Up Hope"; "Guilt—The Gift That Keeps on Giving"; "One Day I Shall Burst My Buds of Calm and Blossom into Hysteria"; and "My Future's So Bright I Gotta Wear Shades."

Miller, Donald. *Blue Like Jazz: Nonreligious Thoughts on Christian Spirituality.* Nashville: Thomas Nelson, 2003.

> I'd like to say, "If you understand jazz, you'll like Donald Miller." However, I don't understand jazz at all, but I love Donald Miller. He inspires the one who wants to grow in Christ to think outside the box.

Miller, Donald, *Searching for God Knows What.* Nashville: Thomas Nelson, 2004.

> This is a fresh, slightly irreligious look at faith from someone who looks at God honestly and with refreshing candor.

FAMILY

Arp, David, Claudia Arp, and John and Margaret Bell. *Loving Your Relatives Even When You Don't See Eye-to-Eye.* Wheaton, IL: Tyndale, 2003.

> We all struggle with relatives. We all have family get-togethers, family holidays, family reunions. This resource helps us to get through them—and get through them well.

Balswick, Jack O., and Judith K Balswick. *The Family: A Christian Perspective on the Contemporary Home.* Grand Rapids, MI: Baker, 2007.

> The Balswicks give a solidly Christian view of the family. They look at biblical truths and sociological information from their perspective as therapists.

Curran, Dolores. *Traits of a Healthy Family.* New York: Random House, 1984.

> So often Christians focus on the dysfunctional family; this book looks at the healthy family. Curran has come up with fifteen qualities that experts attribute to a healthy family.

Stoop, David, and James Masteller. *Forgiving Our Parents, Forgiving Ourselves: Healing Adult Children of Dysfunctional Families.* Ann

Arbor, MI: Servant, 1997.

> For the person who comes from a dysfunctional family, this book gives a step-by-step approach to identifying, understanding, and moving beyond that dysfunction.

Swindoll, Charles R. *The Strong Family*. Grand Rapids, MI: Zondervan, 1994.

> Swindoll's understandable, Christ-centered, biblical approach in this book on the family helps build relationships based on wisdom and mutual respect.

Weidmann, Jim, Janet Weidmann, and Otis and Gail Ledbetter. *Spiritual Milestones: A Guide to Celebrating Your Children's Spiritual Passages*. Colorado Springs, CO: David C. Cook, 2001.

> Christian leaders today have begun to realize that because of the fast pace of our culture, with all its emptiness and error, we must be intentional in sharing our love for Christ with the next generation. The Weidmanns and the Ledbetters have expanded on this challenge with practical suggestions for parents to celebrate their children's spiritual passages — much as Jewish homes celebrate rite of passage into manhood and womanhood.

FORGIVENESS

Sande, Ken. *The Peacemaker: A Biblical Guide to Resolving Personal Conflict*. Grand Rapids, MI: Baker, 2004.

> Reconciliation is the goal for conflict resolution. Matthew 18 tells us to go to our brother and reconcile. This book guides us through that process.

Smedes, Lewis B. *Shame and Grace: Healing the Shame We Don't Deserve*. New York: HarperCollins, 1993.

> Dr. Smedes identifies shame as what it really is — a robber of our joy in Christ! He looks at the symptoms, the healing, and the Healer who gives us His grace.

Tournier, Paul. *Guilt and Grace*. San Francisco: Harper & Row, 1983.
In this book, Tournier takes another look at guilt, which can either lead us to grace or keep us from experiencing the joy of that grace.

GRIEF

Jeremiah, David. *A Bend in the Road: Experiencing God When Your World Caves In*. Nashville: Thomas Nelson, 2002.
The beauty of this book is that it raises us above our grief and loss to see God's provision, comfort, presence, and encouragement.

Sittser, Gerald L. *A Grace Disguised*: *How the Soul Grows Through Loss*. Grand Rapids, MI: Zondervan, 1995.
In this excellent resource on grief and loss, Gerald Sittser tells his own story — the death of his wife, his daughter, and his mother — and then helps readers understand their own grief. Whatever that grief may be, Sittser helps us see the biblical principles that apply.

Swindoll, Charles. *For Those Who Hurt*. Grand Rapids, MI: Zondervan, 1977.
With this book, Swindoll helps prepare us for the pressures of life: heartache, crisis, loss, and pain.

Yancey, Philip. *Disappointment with God*. Grand Rapids, MI: Zondervan, 1992.
While this book deals with loss, the bigger questions addressed here are: "Why, God?" "Why did you allow this?" and "Can we really trust God?" Yancey guides us through our disappointments and our questions.

Zonnenbelt-Smeenge, Susan J., and Robert C. De Vries. *Traveling Through Grief: Learning to Live Again After the Death of a Loved One*. Grand Rapids, MI: Baker, 2006.

Traveling Through Grief is a compassionate resource to help you find your road after the death of a loved one. The unique help in this book comes from the personal experiences of the authors and their own journeys of losing their spouses. They give five specific tasks to work through during the healing process.

HOMOSEXUALITY

Johnson, Barbara. *Where Does a Mother Go to Resign?* Minneapolis: Bethany, 2004.

> What does a mother do when she finds out her son is gay? How does this intersect with her faith? Barbara Johnson shares her struggles with humor and encouragement.

Mickey, Paul A. *Of Sacred Worth.* Nashville: Abingdon, 1991.

> This book looks through the eyes of compassion at the biblical stance on homosexuality, as well as the sacred worth of the person. Mickey addresses that AIDS is not God's judgment on homosexuals. Chapter titles include "We Are Sexual Beings"; "The Purpose of Sexuality Is Intimacy"; "Heterosexual and Homosexual Lifestyles"; "The Old Testament and Homosexuality"; "The New Testament and Homosexuality"; "A Contemporary Debate on Homosexuality in the Church"; and "Homosexuality and the Church's Ministry."

LISTENING

Howe, Reuel L. *The Miracle of Dialogue.* San Francisco: HarperSanFrancisco, 1993.

> Howe helps readers understand the "meeting of meaning" as they learn better communication skills. Chapter titles include "The Importance of Dialogue," "The Barriers to Communication," "From Monologue to Dialogue," "The

Purpose of Dialogue," "The Participants in Dialogue," "The Dialogical Crisis," "The Fruits of Dialogue," and "Dialogue and the Tasks Ahead."

Stanley, Charles. *Listening to God: In Touch Series.* Nashville: Thomas Nelson, 1996.

Most of us would like to be able to say, "Speak, Lord, for your servant listens," just as the boy Samuel said in the Old Testament. God does speak to us—most often we just don't listen. Stanley helps us to understand how to listen to Him and understand.

MARRIAGE

Chapman, Gary. *The Five Love Languages: How to Express Heartfelt Commitment to Your Mate.* Chicago: Northfield, 2007.

Dr. Chapman helps readers identify which of the five love languages is their dominant one, as well as how to discover their partner's primary love language.

Chapman, Gary. *Loving Solutions: Overcoming Barriers in Your Marriage.* Chicago: Moody, 1999.

Finding answers to the obstacles a couple is facing in their marriage is the reason for this book. Little things develop into bigger issues, and Dr. Chapman helps identify and deal with those root issues.

Dobson, James C. *Love Must Be Tough: New Hope for Marriages in Crisis.* Carol Stream, IL: Tyndale, 2007.

Tough times call for tough love. This book is written for those on the brink of divorce and for those dealing with painful relationships.

Hardin, Jerry D., and Dianne C. Sloan. *Getting Ready for Marriage Workbook: How to Really Get to Know the Person You're Going to Marry.* Nashville: Thomas Nelson, 1992.

This workbook delves into the influences a family has on an individual and how your background inevitably affects your marriage.

Parrott, Les, and Leslie Parrott. *Saving Your Marriage Before It Starts*. Grand Rapids, MI: Zondervan, 2006.

The Parrotts have given a gift to couples of all ages who want great marriages. Their insightful, creative, and fun-to-read book is built on proven principles from their counseling, teaching, and seminars.

Peace, Martha. *The Excellent Wife: A Biblical Perspective*. Bemidji, MN: Focus Publishing, 1999.

This book is a good Bible study tool for women wanting to better understand God's plan. It gives a detailed portrait of a godly wife.

Thomas, Gary. *Sacred Marriage*. Grand Rapids, MI: Zondervan, 2000.

Thomas shows how marriage is more than a sacred covenant with another person. It is a spiritual discipline designed to help you know God better, trust Him more fully, and love Him more deeply.

MENOPAUSE

Conway, Sally. *Menopause: Help and Hope for This Passage*. Grand Rapids, MI: Zondervan, 1990.

Speaking out of her own heart and personal experience, Sally Conway takes a thorough look at the journey of menopause. Chapter titles include "First-Time Changes for You," "Our Foremothers." "Your Wonderful Body," "Now That Reproduction Is Over," "The Estrogen Question," "Hysterectomy—Pro and Con," "The Joy—or Pain—of Sex," "Osteoporosis—The Silent Thief," "Combating

Heart Attacks and Other Assaults," "It's Not Just Your
Imagination," and "For Husbands and Children Only."

Demetre, Danna. *The Heat Is On: Health, Humor and Hope for
Women Facing Menopause.* Grand Rapids, MI: Revell, 2005.
> Many myths and jokes surround the difficult stage of meno-
> pause. This book addresses the myths, answers the ques-
> tions, and gives practical suggestions.

MISCARRIAGE

Rank, Maureen. *Free to Grieve: Healing and Encouragement for Those
Who Have Suffered Miscarriage and Stillbirth.* Grand Rapids, MI:
Bethany, 2004.
> This is an encouraging and "normalizing" look at the grief
> of miscarriage. The author talks about the pain—emotional
> and physical—and offers hope for the future.

Vredevelt, Pam. *Empty Arms: Hope and Support for Those Who Have
Suffered a Miscarriage, Stillbirth, or Tubal Pregnancy.* Portland, OR:
Multnomah, 1984.
> Many parents who have experienced the heartbreak of
> miscarriage or stillbirth recommend this book as a helpful
> resource. With the empathy personal experience brings, the
> author is able to gently offer comfort to the woman who has
> just experienced miscarriage or stillbirth as well as insight
> to her friends and family who want to help and encourage
> effectively.

PARENTING

Chapman, Gary, and Ross Campbell. *The Five Love Languages of
Children.* Chicago: Moody, 1997.
> Each person—whether parent or child—has his or her own
> love language. This book helps parents to identify the love

languages of their children and then to communicate and love them best using that language.

Chapman, Gary. *The Five Love Languages of Teenagers*. Chicago: Northfield, 2000.

Sometimes, perhaps most of the time, parents feel their teens speak a foreign language. This book helps parents and teens understand and communicate with one another.

Clark, Chap, and Dee Clark. *Disconnected: Parenting Teens in a MySpace World*. Grand Rapids, MI: Baker, 2007.

Your teens live in a MySpace world with different sorts of challenges than you faced. Chap and Dee Clark can help you understand your teen. They describe how things have changed and give you ideas on how to build your relationship with your teen.

Cline, Foster, and Jim Fay. *Parenting with Love and Logic*. Rev. ed. Colorado Springs, CO: Piñon Press, 2006.

Fay and Cline are gurus in helping parents to teach their kids personal responsibility. Logical consequences follow behavior, and this resource helps parents to establish "healthy control."

Huggins, Kevin. *Parenting Adolescents*. Colorado Springs, CO: NavPress, 1992.

This book helps parents look at their own growing, maturing walk with Christ as they help their teen. Huggins points out opportunities to build godly character through normal, everyday situations.

Secunda, Victoria. *When You and Your Mother Can't Be Friends: Resolving the Most Complicated Relationship of Your Life*. New York: Dell, 1990.

How often have you been told, "You're just like your mother"? For many, that is not a compliment. Secunda examines and deals with the complex mother-daughter relationship.

White, Joe, and Larry Weeden. *Wired by God: Empowering Your Teen for a Life of Passion and Purpose*. Wheaton, IL: Tyndale, 2004.
This is a guidebook for parents to help their teens discover who God made them to be—their own unique God-given blueprint!

Wiggin, Eric. *The Gift of Grandparenting: Building Meaningful Relationships with Your Grandchildren*. Wheaton, IL: Tyndale, 2001.
Rather than being just a source for cookies and zoo trips, this book shows how grandparents can impact a child's life for eternity—whether around the corner or across the country.

PHYSICAL LOSS/CHRONIC PAIN

Hansel, Tim. *You Gotta Keep Dancin': In the Midst of Life's Hurts, You Can Choose Joy!* Colorado Springs, CO: David C. Cook, 1998.
Tim Hansel is an incredible example of growing and deepening in Christlikeness while going through the valley of suffering. Chapter titles include "An Eternal Moment in Time," "A Blessed Rage to Live," "Breakdown or Breakthrough," "Mere Life," "The Advantages of Disadvantages," "Peace Inside the Pain," "Muffled Triumph," and "With Gladness and Hunger."

Sanders, Becki Conway, Jim Conway, and Sally Conway. *What God Gives When Life Takes*. Downers Grove, IL: InterVarsity Press, 1989.
The Conway family shares their struggles and their joys through the amputation of their sixteen-year-old daughter's leg. Chapter titles include "I Helped Make That Leg—A Mother's Perspective," "Dark Day of Despair" "A Different Kind of Miracle," "Working Through a Crisis," "Let God Be

God," "God Doesn't Make Mistakes," "A Crisis Is Unfair," "A Crisis Helps Us Appreciate What We Have," and "A Crisis Gives Us the Ability to Comfort Others."

RAPE

Adams, Caren, and Jennifer Fay. *Free of the Shadows: Recovering from Sexual Violence.* Oakland, CA: New Harbinger, 1990.

>Adams and Fay address adult victims of rape and their friends and family. They offer wise counsel that covers all stages of recovery, not just the initial decision and adjustment states.

Leslie, Kristen J. *When Violence Is No Stranger: Pastoral Counseling with Survivors of Acquaintance Rape.* Minneapolis: Augsburg Fortress, 2002.

>Pulling from her work with numerous survivors, the author helps the pastoral caregiver to better understand the trauma to the victim and family as well as the importance of helping all involved with their own faith journey — their struggles, their questions, their emotions, and their pain.

SEXUAL ADDICTION/PORNOGRAPHY

Carnes, Patrick. *Out of the Shadows: Understanding Sexual Addiction.* Minneapolis: Comp Care, 1983.

>In this "twelve-step" guide to recovery from sexual addiction, the author examines the tangled web of love, addictive sex, hate, and fear usually founded in family relationships. Chapter titles include "The Addiction Cycle," "The Levels of Addiction," "The Family and the Addict's World," "Coaddiction," "The Belief System," "Twelve Steps to Recovery," and "The Future Is Conditional."

Frederick, Dennis, *Conquering Pornography: Overcoming the Addiction*. Enumclaw, WA: Pleasant Word, 2007.

> This book specifically addresses men who admit their addiction to pornography and want to be freed from that addiction.

White, John. *Eros Defiled*. Downers Grove, IL: InterVarsity, 1986.

> The author helps the struggler identify and understand sexual sins. It goes beyond understanding to hope, encouragement, and specific help for healing. Chapter titles include "Sex, Science and Morality"; "Your Urges and How You Experience Them"; "Sex on a Desert Island"; "The Freedom That Enslaves"; "The Scarlet Letter"; "Two Halves Do Not Make One Whole"; and "The Discipline That Heals."

PHONE NUMBERS OF HELPFUL RESOURCES

Aging Issues _____

Alternative Pregnancy Center _____

Cemeteries _____

Debt Counseling Agency _____

Fire Department _____

Free Medical Clinic _____

Homeless Shelters _____

Hospitals _____

Legal Aid _____

Mental Health, County _____

Mortuaries _____

Public Defender's Office _____

Rape Hotline _____

Red Cross _____

Safe House _____

Schools _____

Social Services (or other child abuse

reporting agency) _____

Suicide Hotline _____

Therapists _____

Victim's Assistance (can be found through

local police or sheriff offices) _____

About the Author

BARBARA M. ROBERTS has a degree in pastoral care and family counseling from Regis University, and she has been in the field of caring for those who hurt for many years. Her teaching and speaking, as well as one-on-one caregiving and pastoral counseling, have given her broad experience and exposure to the needs of others. "Listening, sharing in another's pain, and being privileged to pray with that person are a gift that God has given to me. I am blessed to be able to use the gift for what I hope continues to be to His glory."

Barb was called by God at a very young age. Even as a young girl, her heart desired to know God and to serve Him. She is a Colorado native who grew up in the Denver area and has stayed close to home. In 1961, she married her husband, Ken, and her greatest joys involve her family—husband, three children and their amazing spouses, and nine grandchildren.

Additional resources from NavPress to help with tough crises.

Kitchen Table Counseling
Muriel L. Cook and Shelly Cook Volkhardt
978-1-57683-795-5

Join author Muriel Cook as she shares the valuable lessons she's learned throughout her life as a lay counselor, addressing the needs of hurting women from a spiritual perspective. *Kitchen Table Counseling* will prepare you for the fulfilling, vital ministry of encouraging other women to know Christ and trust Him through the difficult experiences of their lives.

No Longer Alone
Sallie Culbreth
978-1-60006-392-3

If you're a survivor of abuse, you know firsthand the feelings of abandonment, betrayal, exposure, and despair. What you might not realize is how fully Jesus knows them too. His abuse began with a kiss. Listen as Jesus explains how He knows dread, betrayal, humiliation, and much more.

Thriving Despite a Difficult Marriage
Michael Misja and Chuck Misja
978-1-60006-214-8

Christian psychologists Michael Misja and Chuck Misja show you how to be free from shame when your marriage is not "successful" by conventional Christian standards. Find a basis for joy and learn how to love from godly strength without asking for a response from your spouse.

To order copies, call NavPress at 1-800-366-7788 or log on to www.navpress.com.